Top Notes

T0360046

Malala Yousafzai & Christina Lamb's

I am Malala

Study notes for Common Module:
Texts and Human Experiences 2019–2023 HSC

Bruce Pattinson & Jane Norris

A
FIVE SENSES
PUBLICATION

Five Senses Education Pty Ltd
2/195 Prospect Highway
Seven Hills 2147
New South Wales
Australia

Pattinson, Bruce
Top Notes – I am Malala
ISBN 978-1-76032-211-3

CONTENTS

TOP NOTES SERIES

This series has been created to assist HSC students of English in their understanding of set texts. Top Notes are easy to read, providing analysis of issues and discussion of important ideas contained in the texts.

Particular care has been taken to ensure that students are able to examine each text in the context of the module it has been allocated to.

Each text generally includes:

- Notes on the specific module
- Plot summary
- Character analysis
- Setting
- Thematic concerns
- Language studies
- Essay questions and a response outline
- Other textual material
- Study practice questions
- Useful quotes

We have covered the areas we feel are important for students in their study of *Texts and Human Experiences* for their Common Module. I am sure you will find these Top Notes useful in your studies of English.

Bruce Pattinson
Series Editor

COMMON MODULE: TEXTS AND HUMAN EXPERIENCES

"It is quite possible—overwhelmingly probable, one might guess—that we will always learn more about human life and personality from novels than from scientific psychology"

NOAM CHOMSKY

What is the Common Module?

The Common Module set for the 2019–23 HSC is *Texts and Human Experiences*. It is compulsory to study this topic as prescribed by NESA and it is common to all three English courses. Remember: you will be learning how texts reveal individual and collective human experiences. There are no right or wrong answers in this module – it is about how you see and interpret material and engage with it.

In the Common Module you will be analysing one prescribed text and a range of short texts that are related to the idea of human experiences. You will analyse texts not only to investigate the ideas they present about this area but also how they convey these ideas. This means you will be looking closely at the techniques a composer uses to represent his / her messages and shape meaning. You will also be looking at relationships between texts in regard to the experiences you explore. Overall, you will become an expert on texts and the human experience — that is, the different notions people have about human experience and the various ways composers manipulate techniques to communicate their ideas about it.

Specifically you will look at one set text from the following list.

- Doerr, Anthony, *All the Light We Cannot See*
- Lohrey, Amanda, *Vertigo*
- Orwell, George, *Nineteen Eighty-Four*
- Parrett, Favel, *Past the Shallows*
- Dobson, Rosemary 'Young Girl at a Window', 'Over the Hill', 'Summer's End', 'The Conversation', 'Cock Crow', 'Amy Caroline', 'Canberra Morning'
- Slessor, Kenneth 'Wild Grapes', 'Gulliver', 'Out of Time', 'Vesper-Song of the Reverend Samuel Marsden', 'William Street', 'Beach Burial'
- Harrison, Jane, *Rainbow's End*
- Miller, Arthur, *The Crucible*
- Shakespeare, William, *The Merchant of Venice*
- Winton, Tim, *The Boy Behind the Curtain* Chapters: 'Havoc: A Life in Accidents', 'Betsy', 'Twice on Sundays', 'The Wait and the Flow', 'In the Shadow of the Hospital', 'The Demon Shark', 'Barefoot in the Temple of Art'
- Yousafzai, Malala & Lamb, Christina, *I am Malala*
- Daldry, Stephen, *Billy Elliot*
- O'Mahoney, Ivan, *Go Back to Where You Came From* – Series 1, Episodes 1, 2 and 3 and *The Response*
- Walker, Lucy, *Waste Land*

NESA has mandated that students must study a related text as part of the common module, and that this should be part of their in-school assessment. However there is NO LONGER a requirement to write about a related text in the HSC examination itself.

WHAT DOES NESA REQUIRE FOR THE COMMON MODULE?

The NESA documentation of the Common Module: Texts and Human Experiences states that students:

- deepen their understanding of how texts represent individual and collective human experiences;

- examine how texts represent human qualities and emotions associated with, or arising from, these experiences;

- appreciate, explore, interpret, analyse and evaluate the ways language is used to shape these representations in a range of texts in a variety of forms, modes and media;

- explore how texts may give insight into the anomalies, paradoxes and inconsistencies in human behaviour and motivations, inviting the responder to see the world differently, to challenge assumptions, ignite new ideas or reflect personally;

- may also consider the role of storytelling throughout time to express and reflect particular lives and cultures;

- by responding to a range of texts, further develop skills and confidence using various literary devices, language concepts, modes and media to formulate a considered response to texts;

- study one prescribed text and a range of short texts that provide rich opportunities to further explore representations of human experiences illuminated in texts;

- make increasingly informed judgements about how aspects of these texts, for example, context, purpose, structure, stylistic and grammatical features, and form shape meaning;

- select one related text and draw from personal experience to make connections between themselves, the world of the text and their wider world;

- by responding and composing throughout the module, further develop a repertoire of skills in comprehending, interpreting and analysing complex texts;

- examine how different modes and media use visual, verbal and/or digital language elements;

- communicate ideas using figurative language to express universal themes and evaluative language to make informed judgements about texts;

- further develop skills in using metalanguage, correct grammar and syntax to analyse language and express a personal perspective about a text

If this is what is required by NESA, we need to examine the concept of human experience carefully so we can adequately respond in these ways. I would recommend that you read the complete document which is on the NESA web site and can be downloaded in Word or Adobe. Understanding this document is an important step in handling the textual material within the guidelines required — remember you are reading for a purpose and should make notes and highlight ideas as you read so that you can develop these ideas later.

UNDERSTANDING THE COMMON MODULE

What are Human Experiences?

The concept of Human Experiences is at the heart of the Common Module.

Human Experiences are experiences of individuals or a group of people (eg a family, society, or nation) in life. There are a very wide range of human experiences which include but go beyond this list:

- feelings or reactions (momentary or long term): love, hate, anger, joy, fear, disgust
- key milestones or stages: birth, childhood, adulthood, marriage, divorce, death
- culture, belonging and identity
- conformity and rebellion
- innocence and guilt, justice
- freedom and repression
- education, vocation, work, sport, leisure
- attraction to a person, idea, group or cause
- opposition to an idea, cause, political system
- religious faith or belief
- extreme events such as an earthquake, avalanche, tsuanami
- regular events such as walking, eating, singing, dancing, discussing ideas.

The word *experience* seems innately connected to the human condition and it is something we have each day whether a mundane experience that is repetitive, or something new and dramatic which offers challenges and rewards. Experiences can vary greatly in their impact on individuals, groups and countries. One example might be a war that is a negative experience for a whole population while we may experience the wonder of medicine with a new vaccine for a deadly disease that saves millions of people. We need to note that the module asks for 'experiences' ...we are a combination of different experiences and each has a varying impact. One person's problem is another's challenge depending on perspective, skill set, previous experience and ability.

Experiences are widespread and often shared: this is why people tell their stories and these shared experiences form part of our cultural heritage. These experiences often inform, warn and teach across entire cultural groups and many stories are shared across cultures.

DEFINING HUMAN EXPERIENCES

Now let's attempt to define what human experiences are and shape them into a more coherent and easily understood framework so we can begin our investigation at a basic level of understanding before moving into more complex analysis and looking at how the texts illuminate our understanding of the term.

Dictionary.com defines the term **experience** as:

noun

1. a particular instance of personally encountering or undergoing something:

2. the process or fact of personally observing, encountering, or undergoing something:

3. the observing, encountering, or undergoing of things generally as they occur in the course of time:
   to learn from experience; the range of human experience.

4. knowledge or practical wisdom gained from what one has observed, encountered, or undergone, e.g. *a man of experience.*

5. *Philosophy.* the totality of the cognitions given by perception; all that is perceived, understood, and remembered.

verb

(used with object), **experienced, experiencing**.

6. to have experience of; meet with; undergo; feel, e.g. *to experience nausea.*

7. to learn by experience.

idiom

8. **experience religion**, to undergo a spiritual conversion by which one gains or regains faith in God.

Obviously there are a number of definitions according to context, but all are applicable to our study in some shape or form, as the range of human experience is so vast. The search for 'new experience' has driven much of the development of people, groups, cultures and nations over past millennia. New experiences are always met with excitement and often trepidation as to what change they might bring.

Think historically about how people have reacted to change. It can cause great upheavals in society, with violent reactions while other changes brought through various experiences are welcomed and may change how people live and comprehend the world. Experiences affect us emotionally in many cases rather than logically and when we respond emotionally, behaviours become unpredictable. This causes the paradoxes, anomalies and inconsistencies mentioned in the rubric. If we were logical beings the world would be an easier place, but probably more boring.

These definitions all point to the fact that memory is the key to experience. The experience is stored in memory and drawn upon when the circumstances are repeated or closely mimicked so we can deal with them — hopefully better than on the initial experience.

Experiences can come in many ways and the synonyms listed below for experience help us to understand the concept even further. They assist in defining how an experience can arise:

Synonyms

actions	understanding	judgment
background	wisdom	observation
contacts	acquaintances	perspicacity
involvement	actuality	practicality
know-how	caution	proofs
maturity	combat	savoir-faire
participation	doings	seasonings
patience	empiricism	sophistication
practice	evidence	strife
reality	existences	trials
sense	exposures	worldliness
skill	familiarity	forebearance
struggle	intimacy	
training	inwardness	

http://www.thesaurus.com/browse/experience?s=t

These synonyms show partly the vast array of words that our language has created around this concept, and also shows how important it is in the human psyche. We, as humans, want to experience. Now we will look at some examples of experiences and examine how they can have an impact. It is also important to remember that experiences do not have to be positive. You might experience a huge problem, a bereavement, a car accident, an unwelcome relationship or something totally bizarre that rocks your world. There can be a more opaque side to any experience that may need to be addressed.

The whole aim of this Common Module is to examine the text closely but also relate it to the concept of human experiences and decide how examining it in this way enables us to better understand both the text and the concept of humanity.

It is important that you unpack what each text you study shows you about human experiences and what ideas / themes arise from those experiences. Formulate your own ideas about the text.

Read the NESA Stage 6 document called *English Stage 6: Annotations of selected texts prescribed for the Higher School Certificate 2019-23* (see *www.educationstandards.nsw.edu.au*) for the set text you are studying. This document offers insights into the way each particular text should be examined by outlining key ideas and areas for clarification.

Human experiences and ways of experiencing vary due to individual circumstance and these experiences can change many things about individual lives, communities and the world. When we examine the concept of human experience in relation to a text, we need to examine the assumptions or biases we bring to it as well as how experiencing the text itself may change us and how we view things. The text may challenge and confront how we view the human experience or we may have preconceived ideas that make it more difficult for this to happen.

Students can also think about their own 'personal experience to make connections between themselves, the world of the text and their wider world.' Examining and enjoying any text is an experience in itself but it is what we take away from the text and apply that is the crucial aspect. That is not to say that every text will be enjoyed or offer a human experience that is significant either positively or negatively. Some texts may not personally engage you and that is fine. This is especially so when you begin to look for other related material that links to *Texts and Human Experiences*. We recommend that you find examples of texts that link but also personally appeal to you so that you can relate empathetically with them.

Individual Human Experiences

The idea of personal experiences is a popular and pervasive concept, especially in the literature of many cultures. Recording personal experiences as a means of sharing wisdom or more mundane daily tasks is part of human nature and we record and relate these experiences frequently. Experiences are recorded and relayed in many ways. We tell oral stories in both anecdotal and formal ways, we write, draw, sing and photograph our way into history (or not). Look at the proliferation of social media in this current century as people record their daily, even hourly, experiences for all to see. We record the most trivial details of our lives for likes and followers while the real world passes us by. Human experiences affect us on a daily basis and some experiences influence our lives and the way we live them.

Individuals seek out experiences in a variety of ways. Some seek more and more extreme experiences to test themselves against the world. Others limit their experiences. A lot of people prefer the familiar and don't actively seek new experiences. Individuals, it must be remembered, also see experiences in different ways and the same experience may have a very different impact on individuals. The one thing we can be certain about is that experiences are part of humanity and even the most limited of us have them. Many of these experiences also come from interaction with others and as noted we also like to share these experiences.

Experiences are what define us in many ways and are what makes us human.

We are going to look at four specific ways that experiences can influence us as people over the next few pages. These are physical, psychological, emotional and intellectual experiences and many experiences are a combination of these.

Physical Experience

The concept of a physical experience is tied into the human experience and part of the collective experience as well. Individuals seek physical experiences to test themselves against nature and other individuals often as part of trials and rituals, for example being integrated into a community. In modern times individuals have sought to test themselves with extreme sports and explorations into the harshest conditions and even space. Physical experiences can also change the way we see the world and others because of the chemical changes these experiences have on our bodies and mind. Physical experiences are often challenges and part of the experience is overcoming adversity. These physical challenges are often celebrated, as in the case of sports, but can also offer challenges if the experience is a negative one such as an accident or disease. Physical experiences are also often quite public and thus have permeated our societies in both their execution and how they are perceived. These physical experiences, even if experienced vicariously, have become popular across cultures and celebrated. Think of examples for yourself but most competitive sports offer examples.

Bruce Lee extends the concept of the physical experience into all aspects of life and that's what we will look at next in our analysis of human experiences –

> *'If you always put limits on everything you do, physical or anything else, it will spread into your work and into your life. There are no limits. There are only plateaus, and you must not stay there, you must go beyond them.'*

Psychological Experience

The idea of a psychological experience is tied into many of the abstract ideas that people experience and can lead to a discussion of what is normal psychology. From the earliest times humans have attempted to alter their psychology through a number of experiences. On a simple level this can be a drug that changes the person's or group's perspective on reality. Examples of this might be alcohol or marijuana but cultural groups also use various substances to share group experiences. This can be seen in Native American cultures with *peyote*. In more modern times prescription drugs that are mood altering have been used to minimise the symptoms of psychiatric illnesses such as depression, and these mood altering drugs are common and legal. Others attempt to alter their psychology by seeing specialists in this area while others act out their condition leading to social and criminal issues. When discussing the human experience, psychology is a key issue and will form a part of most studies of experience. When taken too far this search for a new psychological experience can be harmful eg. an addiction.

Carl Jung, the famous psychologist, comments on the problems of addiction for human experiences, stating clearly that excess can be an issue:

> *"Every form of addiction is bad, no matter whether the narcotic be alcohol, morphine or idealism."*

Emotional Experience

According to the psychologist, Robert Plutchik, there are eight basic emotions:

- **Fear** — feeling afraid.
- **Anger** — feeling angry. A stronger word for anger is rage.
- **Sadness** — feeling sad. Other words are sorrow, grief (a stronger feeling, for example when someone has died) or **depression** (feeling sad for a long time without any external cause). Some people think depression is a different emotion.
- **Joy** — feeling happy. Other words are happiness, gladness.
- **Disgust** — feeling something is wrong or nasty
- **Trust** — a positive emotion; admiration is stronger; **acceptance** is weaker
- **Anticipation** — in the sense of looking forward positively to something which is going to happen. **Expectation** is more neutral; **dread** is more negative.

https://simple.wikipedia.org/wiki/List_of_emotions

Emotions are the strongest drivers of human experience and form lasting aspects of any experience. Think about breaking up with someone you love and the emotions that drive behaviours in this situation. People have all sorts of extreme behaviours under the influence of emotions and these experiences are often the ones recorded and those which influence us most. Think about the role emotions play in our lives and the range of emotions from the list above. Consider how much emotions affect our life experiences, how they influence our decisions which decide our experiences and on a higher level consider how they affect the decisions which may seriously impact our experiences, such as politicians going to war.

Intellectual Experience

The concept of an intellectual experience is linked to decisions and experiences we have based on analysis and logic rather than the emotional choices referred to in the previous section. These intellectual experiences have changed the way we live and how we have seen our world. These experiences have affected the way we as humans have altered our world to suit our needs and lead to all the great advances in human society and thus experiences. Changes in our ideas, beliefs etc. alter the way we interact with the world and often these intellectual changes come at great cost.

Think of the time in Europe when the Church dominated and stopped scientific advances by calling them heresy / witchcraft. Open societies are more open to new ideas and this is what has hastened the pace of intellectual experiences as dominant ideologies fall away. Intellectual advances may not have the excitement that the other types produce but perhaps they have a more lasting impact on people, societies and the world in general. Ideas are powerful experiences and people hold beliefs strongly.

Immanuel Kant stated that:

> *"experience without theory is blind, but theory without experience is mere intellectual play."*

Consider this statement in the light of what we have learnt about human experiences. Are they a combination of many factors or can we isolate experiences into simple forms?

What exactly is a human experience?

The titular question reminds us of the old brainteaser: "If a tree falls in a forest and no one is around to hear it, does it make a sound?"

There are two classic responses to this. The more Platonically-minded would say the tree always makes a sound when it falls in the forest. We don't have to be there to hear it; we can imagine the sound of a tree falling in the forest, based on memory of such an event or on the recording of such an event. We know that sound is just vibrating air, and it's safe to say that air always vibrates in response to a tree falling, or a bear growling, or a cicada singing, whether we are there to hear it or not.

The second answer is a more post-structuralist response: the sound doesn't occur on its own; it needs a human ear to be heard. Therefore, if there is no human in the forest to hear the tree fall, then there is no sound. This automatically implies that "experience" of anything requires the presence of a human being, which means there is no such thing as an experience that *isn't* human.

Animal rights activists – or anyone with a beloved pet – would almost certainly reject this notion because it prioritises humans and relegates all other species to a lower class of being: an attitude that most would agree has gotten the human race into an awful lot of environmental trouble over the last 200 years of industrialisation.

In his article (*What is an Experience?*), my learned colleague Paul Hartley describes experience in its most basic form, as "the perception of something else" and "ultimately information about what we have perceived." But does this make it particularly human? Dogs and cats perceive things. Insects perceive things. You could even say that plants perceive things, such as the direction from which the sun is shining. Perception is the most basic of life's survival tools for all manner of flora and fauna.

In her brief but cogent disquisition on the subject (*What is Human?*), another of my learned colleagues, Nadine Hare, asserts that to be human is a social construct. Hartley builds on that notion by suggesting that culture affects experience when we start to share it, because "the words, associations, and priorities we attach to the shared experience define how we understand the world we live in."

Hare rightly points out that this world is increasingly dominated by consumerism, which has distorted what it means to be human by excluding all of the attributes and qualities that "make people people." Calling us consumers reduces our experiences to mere transactions. It defines human experience within the narrow confines of the purchase funnel and has little interest in anything that isn't a purchase driver.

Perhaps the field of commerce is where the experiential rubber most emphatically meets the road. Unlike mere perception, commerce is a uniquely human experience. It has mediated, automated, and dominated the human agenda to the point where we are defined by what we buy and little else. Commerce has invaded the non-profit spheres of government, health, and education, imposing its own priorities and principles on these institutions in the expectation that they will behave more like businesses. And even though business still strives to appeal to the so-called masses, it prioritises the pursuit of individual wealth, and in so doing, not only inhibits the desire for shared experience but unravels the social fabric historically woven by the democratic tradition.

As if in response, that social fabric is being re-woven by our networks. As Hare asserts, "humans both produce technology and are produced through technology." Experience is shared more now than it ever has been because the experiential platform – i.e., that very human invention called the internet – is in place to facilitate it like never before, and on a global scale.

This sharing capability reintroduces all of those things that "make people people" back into the conversation – whether commercial or political. What "makes people people" is messy, unpredictable, emotional, and complex. Most of what makes us human has no place in the experiential confines of the purchase funnel, and defies any of our attempts to place it there.

The challenge for us as a species is to embrace this new capacity for sharing to keep the agendas of our hegemonic institutions – whether commercial or political – from defining what makes an experience human. A post-consumer business strategy might be one that, as Hare hopes, will "expand our view of people to include the complex and dynamic social, cultural, gendered, spiritual and racialised beings that they are." Maybe then will our shared human experience truly become, as Hartley asserts, the glue that holds us all together as human beings.

Will Novosedlik
MISC magazine

https://miscmagazine.com/what-is-a-human-experience/

This article appeared in the September 2014 edition of MISC magazine. Can you relate to what the article says about human experiences? Do human experiences depend on perception? Does the experience of anything require the presence of a human as experiencer (para 3)? Can the ideas of experience be extended to include perception by plants or animals? Hartley's idea is that "shared human experience" is "the glue that holds us all together as human beings". Is this an oversimplification?

The Impact of Human Experiences

Human experiences have impacts on many levels. On an individual level, we can have changes in our assumptions about the world and people around us; we can ingest new ideas and have these open new vistas of productivity and performance. We can also reflect and build on these experiences to ensure that they are even more meaningful to our lives. Behaviours towards others and the way we respond to the world can manifest themselves in new and different responses. An example might be that through adverse experiences we can build resilience so that the next negative experience isn't as traumatic and we accept it for what it is. Experiences also teach us new behaviours on a very physical level — if you burn yourself once on a flame you learn not to do it again (hopefully).

The impact of human experiences can also be shared in groups and societies. Firstly, let's examine some group dynamics that can be affected by human experiences. Groups share experiences and adapt and develop behaviours that impact on the group as a whole. Think about the notorious 'bonding' sessions sporting teams have that unite them in a common goal. Think about the behaviours of various gangs in our society. We see plenty of examples of this on American television where gangs based on ethnicity and social groupings form specific sets of behaviours that impact on how they interact with each other and the world. These groupings carry assumptions about how they see the world and respond to it. For example, they may have generally negative reactions to law enforcement and this is ingrained into their codes of behaviour. They are suspicious of the world and the people in it — dividing them up into threats, the law and victims. These behaviours are often reinforced by group experiences such as the initiation rituals which are integral to membership.

Often the impact of these behaviours is to perpetuate stereotypes that then categorise the individuals within these groups. The graphic I have included here shows a stereotypical gang member with the suspicious gaze, ubiquitous hoody and scruffy look. These stereotypes reject new ideas and maintain assumptions about the world, often to the detriment of their members. The experiences they have reinforce their own stereotypical way of viewing anything outside the safety of the group and the cycle continues. Of course, other groups have more positive impacts and see the world as a very different place and their experiences are designed to be positive interactions. Think about groups such as Rotary who are constructive in the community. Other groups have specialty interests such as Animal Welfare, Surf Lifesaving and charities.

Normal social interactions impact groups and individuals, but it takes a major event to alter the behaviours of whole societies, especially so in the modern world where societies are large in scale. Earlier in human history smaller experiences could alter the behaviour of societies as they were insignificant in size compared to modern ones. We often fail to remember that many of these ancient societies' behaviours were impacted by superstition, religions and cultural habituation. The modern society as we know it is only a recent phenomenon. Just a few hundred years ago with church rule people were forced to think in a specific

way and punished for not adhering to a theological culture. Think of the Spanish Inquisition, the imprisonment of Galileo and other such restrictions on freedom of thought; scientific breakthroughs were hidden or declared witchcraft. Even recently the world has seen societies kept repressed by failed ideologies. The brutality of such regimes has left deep scars on the social psyche of nations as they try to recover. This has had an impact on the human experiences of whole populations, and societies respond accordingly.

One example might be at the conclusion of the Communist regime in East Germany when the Berlin Wall was destroyed as a visual symbol of the new-found freedom of a whole population of people who had been repressed for decades by a brutal and ever-present regime. Many citizens who had grown up in this system, where you could 'disappear' without trial or real evidence, found the idea that you could express yourself incredible. Many of the

East Germans couldn't believe that this freedom was real and that the Stasi (the secret police) were gone.

Other experiences can affect societies in extreme ways. Think about wars and the impact they have on civilian populations.

Climatic events such as earthquakes change the way that people behave and respond to situations. Catastrophic flooding occurred in the US city of New Orleans in 2005. The US President's response to help was not immediate and the national administration was severely criticised for lack of effective action.

Societies also respond to perceived problems such as pollution. In 1989 the oil tanker Exxon Valdez ran aground in Prince William Sound, Alaska with disastrous results. The effects of this event are still being experienced thirty years later.

Societies can be divided, as we saw with the election of Donald Trump in the United States of America and the reaction of the Political Left.

The impact of human experiences on societies can be quite dramatic, as we have seen, while other experiences (such as an election) can go by without a murmur from societies, no matter who wins. As a last thought before we move on you should also consider the impact of the media on societies in the modern world, and how they influence individuals, societies and the development of ideas.

Problems With Human Behaviour

So far, we have discussed the impact of human experiences on behaviour. Now we can begin to develop some more complex judgements and understandings about the impact of those experiences on human behaviours. In simplistic terms it could be assessed as:

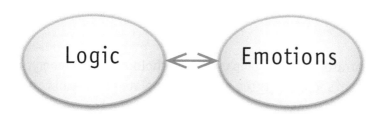

These two opposites on the continuum certainly shape the manner in which we see incidents and how they affect the experience. For instance, if someone you love has no interest in you, it creates a very different reaction to someone you don't care about having no interest in you. It is generally agreed that humans respond more strongly with emotion than they do with logic. Often, it is only through time and reflection that we can understand how an experience has changed and/or altered the manner in which we see a situation or individual.

The Role of Storytelling in Human Experiences

Storytelling has been part of the human experience since 'people' began communicating and it is a method used to convey information and experience as well as be entertaining. Earliest myths were all oral and then people began to write down stories so they weren't lost in time. From this, various theories have developed around storytelling and one is the 'monomyth', which is a template across cultures for storytelling. Let's have a look at this below.

'In narratology and comparative mythology, the monomyth, or the hero's journey, is the common template of a broad category of tales that involve a hero who goes on an adventure, and in a decisive crisis wins a victory, and then comes home changed or transformed.

The concept was introduced in *The Hero with a Thousand Faces* (1949) by Joseph Campbell, who described the basic narrative pattern as follows:

> "A hero ventures forth from the world of common day into a region of supernatural wonder: fabulous forces are there encountered and a decisive victory is won: the hero comes back from this mysterious adventure with the power to bestow boons on his fellow man."

Campbell and other scholars, such as Erich Neumann, describe narratives of Gautama Buddha, Moses, and Christ in terms of the monomyth. Critics argue that the concept is too broad or general to be of much use in comparative mythology. Others say that the hero's journey is only a part of the monomyth; the other part is a sort of different form, or colour, of the hero's journey.

https://en.wikipedia.org/wiki/Hero%27s_journey

Storytelling in History and its Purpose in Human Experience

Storytelling in oral form was accompanied by some theatrics to make the stories as entertaining as possible. Many of the early narratives were based upon religious ceremonies and stories of the creation of the earth and people(s). As time moved on, these stories were accompanied by dance, music and / or theatre and often were part of lengthy rituals, often taking days. These stories were designed to bring meaning to people's lives by explaining their own existence and the purpose / meaning of life in a time when life expectancy was short and entertainment was scarce. Of course stories were also recorded as these experiences were significant to all people and these stories run across all cultures. Before writing, stories were recorded in pictures such as cave art, in tattoo designs on skin and in designs such as rock piles and the giant carved heads of Easter Island.

Writing changed the manner in which stories were told and many of the old oral traditions were lost, barely being kept alive by specialists. Stories began to travel across cultural and national boundaries on whatever surface could be created. Papyrus, bones, pottery, skins, paper and in more modern times film, video and digital storage have changed, over time, the way in which stories of human experience have been told and shared. Content evolved from myth, fable and legend to history, personal narratives and commentary. Modern narrative form often has an educational or didactic element and can drift into propaganda. Stories of self-revelation can be instructive and give audiences the opportunity to apply learning to individual lives, whereas historically narrative was used in this way for societies and groups as a whole. In recent times narratives have become interactive and audiences can choose how the narrative unfolds.

Whatever form the story takes we all have a seemingly innate need for narratives to make sense of our lives. They either confirm our world view or alter our world view depending on the experience they convey and the experiences that we bring to the narrative. We need to remember that narratives are important to human experience and have been significant since the beginning of time.

The Text as an Experience

The concept of the text as an experience is one area to consider as we look at *Texts and Human Experiences*. Reading or viewing the text is an experience in itself and when we do this we bring our own history (experiences) to the text and this helps shape our understanding.

Think about the personal perspective that you bring to a text. What are some of your experiences that might influence how you read a particular text? Some texts, especially personal narratives of trial and tribulation or loss, can be confronting to some audiences and bring back strong opinions or emotions. Many texts attempt to do this as they convey a particular point of view about the world.

Does what you bring to the text affect what you learn from that text? We also need to delve into how the narrative experience is conveyed and how this in turn impacts upon the manner in which the story is received by audiences across different cultures. For example, Western films where heroes fight Islamic terrorism may well be viewed very differently by audiences in Western democracies and Islamic countries. Even seemingly innocuous narratives like the movie 'The Red Pill' which is about men's rights and created by a woman, has caused a polarisation of views wherever it has been shown. Strong personal experiences and viewpoints certainly bring their own understandings to texts.

Questions for Texts and Human Experiences

- Define the module in your own words.
- How are people connected by shared experiences?
- How might physical experience(s) change the way you respond to the world?
- How do you think a person's context and prior experiences shape how they perceive the world?
- Are experiences unique or do prior experiences have an impact on a current experience and way of seeing life?
- What is positive about human experiences?
- Discuss what is negative about human experiences.
- To what extent does experience shape the way we see other people and / or groups?
- Is an individual's culture part of their experience or is it something else?
- Is it possible not to have any meaningful experiences at all?
- Why do people tell stories?
- What do you think you might learn from a narrative?

STUDYING A NON-FICTION TEXT

The medium of a text is very important. If a text is non-fiction this means that its purpose is to report events, situations or trends. It is not created as a novel is; the composer does not choose the events of the story; the events have actually happened. Rather, the composer shapes the text by choosing which events to include and how he or she will portray them. The manner of this portrayal will depend on the composer's purpose. The composer adds his or her perspective to the description of the events. This bias will have an effect on the way the responder perceives the story. The responder can choose to accept or reject the composer's **version** of events.

Realism is created in a non-fiction text by the inclusion of actual people, events or situations. These may be reported objectively or subjectively.

Like the composers of fiction texts, the creator of a non-fiction text creates interest by the use of **language techniques**. These are the elements of the text which are manipulated by the composer to present their ideas effectively. When you are discussing how the composer represents their ideas, you MUST discuss language techniques. Language techniques are sometimes referred to as **stylistic devices**.

The language techniques used in non-fiction are identical to those used in fiction.

LANGUAGE TECHNIQUES

Setting – *where does the action take place? Why? Does the setting have symbolic meaning?*

Main Character portrayal/development: *How does the character develop?* **What is the reader to learn from this?**

Minor Character use: *How does the author use the minor characters represent ideas about themes or major characters*

Narrative Person: *what is the effect this has on the narrative and the reader's response to it?*

LANGUAGE TECHNIQUES

Humour

Symbols and motifs: *how is repetition of image/idea used to maximise the novel's effect?*

Images: *similes, metaphors, personificati*

Dialogue: *not just what is said but how it is important in representing ideas*

Tone: *not just of character comments but also of the narration*

Conflict: *the action, Man vs man, Man vs nature, and/or Man vs himself*

Aural techniques: *Alliteration, assonance, onomatopoeia and rhythm*

WHAT IS A MEMOIR?

I am Malala is generally categorised as a 'memoir' because it is non-fiction and autobiographical in nature and focuses on particular events in Malala's life and in her home country, Pakistan.

A memoir is an historical account of a certain moment in time written from personal knowledge. Often looking back in time, a memoir may offer a degree of reflection and analysis of the events or circumstances which have occurred.

A memoir (US: /ˈmemwɑːr/); from *French*: mémoire: memoria, meaning memory or reminiscence) is a collection of memories that an individual writes about moments or events, both public or private, that took place in the subject's life. The assertions made in the work are understood to be factual.

While memoir has historically been defined as a subcategory of *biography* or *autobiography,* since the late 20th century, the genre is differentiated in form, presenting a narrowed focus. A biography or autobiography tells the story *of a life*, while a memoir often tells a story *from a life*, such as *touchstone* events and turning points from the author's life.

Wikipedia entry

There is a series of articles on *I am Malala* published by the Global Women's Institute at George Washington University and one of these focuses on 'Memoir as Literature and History'. Download and read this to understand the particular choice of a memoir and why that helps make it a more powerful means of expression than other literary forms:

https://malala.gwu.edu/sites/g/files/zaxdzs1061/f/Theme=1.pdf

The author of this article, Julie Donovan states:

> A memoir can excel in evoking immediacy and veracity, where private feelings mesh with public issues and raw emotions intertwine with the detachment of rational argument and the exegesis of an intellectual or political stance. Memoir differs from autobiography in that the memoir concerns a specific, concentrated period within a life, whereas an autobiography tends to recount the story of a life that is generally more all-embracing, with a greater chronological sweep and more linear structure. p3

> Despite Malala's courage, maturity, and poise, her experiences happened when she was a child. Malala's narrative is typical of the memoir's ability to give us an insider's perspective on events that may seem remote when reported in newscasts and other media. The vividness of personal experience evokes not only the sense of terror and displacement caused by Taliban control but also the beauty of the Swat Valley and the renowned hospitality of the Pashtun people. It also serves to educate us about an area too often conceptualised in the abstract. As Malala explains, she thinks of herself as primarily Swati, then Pashtun, and then Pakistani, demonstrating complicated allegiances in regional and national identity. Malala's authorial voice is alternately strident and playful ... p4

You may also like to read this article 'What is a memoir?'
https://bookriot.com/2018/02/16/what-is-a-memoir/

Questions on Memoir

1. Consider how a memoir can help shape our understanding of particular events. How do they differ from other literary forms (eg novel, autobiography)?
2. What key things did you learn from *I am Malala* about Pakistan, its history and political situation?

THE AUTHOR

The story of Malala Yousafzai is well documented in this story and the biographical details are clear for the contributing author Christina Lamb so that material won't be repeated here. It may be interesting for you to get some other perspectives on Malala and so if you go to the following websites they contain information and ideas about her and the memoir.

All site references are correct at time of publication.

This is the obligatory Wikipedia site which is quite good:
https://en.wikipedia.org/wiki/Malala_Yousafzai

Here we have some of the criticism that Malala refers to in the text clearly delineated and this shows how the experiences that Malala has undergone can be interpreted very differently from various political and religious perspectives.

> 'Reception of Yousafzai in Pakistan is mixed. *Dawn* columnist Huma Yusuf summarised three main complaints of Yousafzai's critics: "Her fame highlights Pakistan's most negative aspect (rampant militancy); her education campaign echoes Western agendas; and the West's admiration of her is hypocritical because it overlooks the plight of other innocent victims, like the casualties of U.S. drone strikes." Another *Dawn* journalist, Cyril Almeida, addressed the public's lack of rage against the Tehrik-i-Taliban Pakistan (TTP), blaming the failing state government. Journalist Assed Baig described her as being used to justify Western imperialism as "the perfect candidate for the white man to relieve his burden and save the native". Yousafzai was also accused on social media of being a CIA spy.'

Other sites which are quite factual include:

Biography.com:
https://www.biography.com/people/malala-yousafzai-21362253

Nobel Prize site:
https://www.nobelprize.org/nobel_prizes/peace/laureates/2014/yousafzai-bio.html

Malala Fund:
https://www.malala.org/malalas-story

Time Magazine – this one has a video of Malala speaking at the UN and her speech when she won the Nobel Prize.
http://time.com/3482434/malala-yousafzai-wins-nobel-peace-prize/

CONTEXT

Photo used under Commons Licence: thanks to 'Simon Davis/DFID'.

Pakistan's history is a relatively modern one as a state but the various areas included in its boundaries have a long and varied history. The British partitioned India along religious lines in August 1947 with the Hindu region becoming India and the Muslim areas Pakistan and later Bangladesh (1971). These divisions caused much dislocation of people and it is estimated that up to two million people died in the aftermath of the new border being established along the Radcliffe Line. These dissensions have been a constant cause of angst between the two nations ever since.

The creation of Pakistan began in violence and little has changed since that time. Immigration has continued since that time from Muslims leaving India and this is especially so after the wars with India, all of which were lost, as we read in the text. The war of 1971 was especially violent and caused much consternation in Pakistan, leading to the establishment of Bangladesh. While Pakistan was created in the name of Islam religious tensions have long played a part in its political life as has the army, which is one of the largest in the world.

We read in the text how the tensions between the Sunni and Shia Muslims began to increase with the coming to power of General Zia who wanted a pure Islamic state and we can understand this from the following,

> 'On 5 July 1977, General Zia-ul-Haq led a coup d'etat against Bhutto. Zia-ul-Haq committed himself to establishing an Islamic state and enforcing *sharia* law. Zia established separate Shariat judicial courts and court benches to judge legal cases using Islamic doctrine. New criminal offences (of adultery, fornication, and types of blasphemy), and new punishments (of whipping, amputation, and stoning to death), were added to Pakistani law. Interest payments for bank accounts were replaced by "profit and loss" payments. *Zakat* charitable donations became a 2.5% annual tax. School textbooks and libraries were overhauled to remove un-Islamic material. Offices, schools, and factories were required to offer praying space. Zia bolstered the influence of the *ulama* (Islamic clergy) and the Islamic parties, whilst conservative scholars became fixtures on television. Thousands of activists from the Jamaat-e-Islami party were appointed to government posts to ensure the continuation of his agenda after his passing. Conservative *ulama* (Islamic scholars) were added to the Council of Islamic Ideology. Separate electorates for Hindus and Christians were established in 1985 even though Christian and Hindu leaders complained that they felt excluded from the county's political process.'

> *https://en.wikipedia.org/wiki/Pakistan#Role_of_Islam_
> in_Pakistan*

The tensions between various groups are high and as we read in *I Am Malala* internal fighting and systemic violence is common. When we read the text Malala points to the coups that have seized power from the democratically elected governments and the inadequacy of the army to fight the Taliban and restore order. More recently the government has tried to act and began to address schooling issues and the problem of radicalisation in some mosque schools.

Pakistan is considered a developing nation which belies its historical wealth. Its people(s) have a long history and deep seated culture that goes back centuries. The Pakistani diaspora is the sixth largest in the world and they send much wealth back to the country to support relatives.

This increasing engagement with the world has seen some changes, specifically in the role of women.

'The relationship of women to the opposite gender is culturally that of gender subordination. Women are traditionally assigned, or assumed to have, certain roles related mainly to domestic chores while men are considered the breadwinners and professionals of the family. In urban areas of the country, more and more women are assuming professional roles and contributing to family economics, but the ratio of these women compared with those in traditional roles is small. The occupations most favoured by females and acceptable to society are teaching and tutoring. Due to heightened awareness among people, educational opportunities for Pakistani women have increased over the years. On 24 February 2016, the elected assembly of Pakistan's Punjab province passed a new law called "Punjab Protection of Women Against Violence Bill 2015", which provides women with protection against a multitude of crimes including cyber-crime, domestic violence, and emotional, economic and psychological abuse.'

https://en.wikipedia.org/wiki/Pakistan#Role_of_Islam_in_Pakistan

For more information on Pakistan:

http://www.pakistan.gov.pk/

https://www.cia.gov/library/publications/the-world-factbook/geos/pk.html

https://www.amnesty.org/en/countries/asia-and-the-pacific/pakistan/report-pakistan/

PURPOSE OF *I AM MALALA*

I am Malala is set in a particular cultural and political context in Pakistan during the period of Malala's first 16 years (1997 to 2013). As many readers around the world may be unfamiliar with this, Malala helpfully weaves in details of this context as well as her Pashtun culture in an informative and accessible way.

During this period, Pakistan endured major natural disasters (earthquake and flooding) and enormous political upheaval and violence with the Taliban's uprising in her local area of Swat. Alongside this it is helpful to understand that the context was impacted by the rise of the Taliban in neighbouring Afghanistan during the Cold War.

A helpful article on the context of *I am Malala* in terms of Cultural Politics, Gender and History can be found at this link: *https://malala.gwu.edu/sites/g/files/zaxdzs1061/f/Theme-3-Culture_FINAL.pdf*

The broad purpose of the book can be inferred from the text, *I am Malala*. It is a personal memoir of Malala's young life and it can also be seen as a broader manifesto, calling passionately for girls (and boys) to be educated around the world.

In a statement released by Malala's British publisher prior to its release, Malala said she wrote the book 'to reveal and help children across the world who still struggle to get to school ... I want it to be part of the campaign to give every boy and girl the right to go to school. It is their basic right' *https://abcnews.go.com/International/pakistani-teen-malala-yousafzai-author-book/story?id=18830548*

The book was published one year after she was shot in the head by the Taliban. This event received international attention and brought much publicity to her cause.

SUMMARY

I Am Malala is subtitled *The Girl Who Stood Up for Education and Was Shot by the Taliban* and is the story of a young Pakistani girl, Malala Yousafzai, who is a girls' education campaigner. This non-fiction text has won many awards including Non-fiction Book of the Year while Malala won the Nobel Peace prize for her work. We begin with a graphic of her hand showing calculus and chemical formulae instead of traditional henna designs and then a map of Pakistan and its surrounds to orientate the reader. An enlarged section of the map shows Swat and indicates places of import in the text. The book is dedicated 'To all the girls who have faced injustice and been silenced. Together we will be heard'.

Preface

The preface to this edition (2014) reveals the changes in the two years since the shooting and the year since the book was first published. Malala now lived in Birmingham, England with her family and life had similarities and differences to her life in Pakistan. She wrote about her mother's newfound confidence through education, the wet English weather, the schooling system, her hope to return home one day and her fight 'against ignorance and terrorism'.

Malala's life was very busy and she talked passionately about her role as an education activist, of her family's adjustment, the extensive travel, missing Swat, the positive reception of the book, and her own travels to places such as Kenya and Nigeria. She also discussed the Malala Fund through which she met President Obama in the White House. Finally she talked about meeting Syrian refugees in Jordan and how she too is 'a refugee'.

Prologue – The Day the World Changed

Malala set the context of her present state by reflecting back on her shooting. She stated again that she missed Pakistan and Swat despite all that has happened. The day, 'Tuesday, 9 October 2012' began 'like any other' with Malala waking up, getting ready and catching the bus to school. Malala used to walk to school but had changed to catching the bus due to her mother's fears for her safety. Malala was also aware that something could happen to her.

The bus was 'hot and sticky' and on the way to school it was pulled over. A man came around the back and asked for Malala. He then lifted a Colt 45 and fired 'three shots' one of which 'went through my left eye socket and out under my left shoulder'. The rest of the story is set up in the final sentence:

'Who is Malala? I am Malala and this is my story.' p6

PART ONE: BEFORE THE TALIBAN

1. A Daughter is Born

Malala's birth was met with commiseration from her village because she was a girl and Pakistan was a land where 'daughters are hidden away behind a curtain, their role in life simply to prepare food and give birth to children'. Her father loved her despite the fact she was a girl and she was named after 'Malalai of Maiwand, the greatest heroine of Afganistan'. All Pashtun children learnt about Malalai, who inspired the Afghan army to defeat the British army in 1880.

The Swat Valley 'is the most beautiful place in all the world' and was once independent. Malala's family lived in Mingora, 'the biggest town in the valley' and Islam arrived in the area in the 11th century after Buddhism. The place had many Buddhist relics many of which were later destroyed by the Taliban. Malala's house was one storey and 'proper concrete'. The women gathered on the back porch and Malala liked the roof where she could see the mountains and dream.

When Malala was young the family were very poor and had little. In their culture everyone had a nick-name and hers were *'Pisho'* and *'Lachi'*. Her father had quite dark skin and he had been self-conscious about it but was now content with it because of his marriage. Her mother and father had been married, unlike most, for love and the union was initially problematic because of the families. Malala liked the lifestyle of her family and their gatherings with guests.

Malala's ancestors came from Kabul, Afghanistan, to the Swat Valley in the sixteenth century. Her story includes a significant amount of history of the Pashtun people and their culture. The area, once independently run by a Khan(king), became the North-West Frontier Province of Pakistan and was now known as Khyber Pakhtunkhwa. Malala saw herself 'as Swati and then Pashtun, before Pakistani'. The tradition of the area was that women stayed inside and needed a male relative to go out. Malala wanted things to be different and 'free' but she wondered 'how free a daughter could ever be'.

2. My Father the Falcon

Malala's father Ziauddin had a stutter. Courageously, he entered a public speaking competition with the intention of eliminating his stutter. He taught himself to memorise powerful speeches written by his grandfather, a famous speechmaker. Ziauddin was educated, like all the boys in his family, but the sisters stayed home 'just waiting to be married'. They even got less food. His father had studied in India and seen the creation of Pakistan and the military coups that followed as well as the death of Bhutto.

It was the first coup leader General Zia who 'launched a campaign of Islamisation' to garner popular support. This made the mullahs important and the life of women 'became much more restricted'. For example, a woman's evidence in a court of law was only counted as half of the evidence of a man. Zia even had the history texts rewritten and made Islamic studies compulsory. Then the Russians invaded Afghanistan and there was a flow of refugees into Pakistan. This also made Zia a friend of the Americans in the Cold War as well as gaining him support in the Arab world. The clerics called for 'jihad' and many went to fight the Russians. Malala's father nearly got involved in the jihad but was too intelligent and questioning. He did, however, become political and was 'torn between the two extremes, secularism and socialism on one side and militant Islam on the other'.

Ziauddin worked hard to do well at school and he grew to be a 'very generous man' who used the 'gift of education' well. His pride was boosted by his win in the public speaking which made his hard and frugal father smile. His father started to call him a 'falcon' but he called himself by his clan name 'Ziauddin Yousafzai' as he realised the falcon is a cruel bird.

3. Growing Up in a School

Malala's mother didn't last a term in school and she sold her books for lollies. She couldn't see the point. She regretted this later when she met Malala's father. He 'believed that lack of education was the root of all Pakistan's problems'. Ziauddin had a difficult time getting to college as he had no money. Teaching in Pakistan was corrupt and poorly paid, but eventually he found a place to stay and attend daily.

His arrival at college was around the same time as General Zia was killed in a 'mysterious plane crash' and Benazir Bhutto won the election, the first female Prime Minister of Pakistan and also the first in a Muslim country. Malala's father became involved in student politics and debates in college.

Ziauddin is able to see beyond a *fatwa* (religious ruling) against the controversial book *The Satanic Verses* (by Salman Rushdie) arguing in a student debate 'Is Islam such a weak religion that it cannot tolerate a book written against it? Not my Islam!' This action brought him into conflict with the mullahs: the fatwa had been issued by the Ayatollah Khomeini who had called for

Salman Rushdie's assassination because the book was judged to be blasphemous.

After he, Ziauddin graduated he worked as an English teacher in a private college but the pay was so low he began his own school with a friend. It was a difficult business and they soon split up and another friend stepped in. It was called the Khushal School after a warrior poet from the area. He wanted the students to be warriors with pens, not swords.

The school struggled and Ziauddin ran into corruption but refused to pay the bribes to register the school. He joined an Association of Private Schools with 15 members, became president of the association and expanded its membership to include 400 principals. Adding to his burden, he married and he and his wife eventually lived together in Mingora. The first baby was stillborn and the school continued to lose money. Then it flooded, and their home and the school were destroyed. Then Malala was born and it seemed that their luck changed. They moved into rooms above the school and the school finally began to break even.

Then in 2001 '9/11 would change our world too, and would bring war into our valley'. (p46)

4. The Village

Malala's grandfather, 'Baba', lived in the village known as Barkana. Malala loved her grandfather, and whenever they visited Barkana, Baba would greet her with a song. They always returned to the village for the Eid holidays and the bus trip was an adventure in itself with much to see on the way to the mountains. The area is a big valley with little valleys branching off. In Barkana, the houses were mud and stone and it was an early start for the women who prepared the breakfast. There was no electricity but Malala loved the nature around the 'forgotten place'.

The village had nothing and politicians came, made promises and went. Bribes were the best way to get votes and only the men voted. The girls would go down to the river in groups and play 'weddings'. Sometimes in the village there were real weddings which would be expensive for the families because of the feasting. The older women would tell stories at night to scare the children but as the children got older the village became boring.

Women had to cover their faces in public and couldn't speak to men. Malala was harassed as she didn't cover her face and thought that the Pashtun 'code of conduct' had a 'lot to answer for' especially in regard to women. There were some examples of the horrific treatment of women (pgs 54-5) and things unbelievably were still harder for women in Afghanistan under the Taliban. Now the Taliban were just around the corner and Malala was not aware of the 'clouds gathering' (impending danger).

5. Why I Don't Wear Earrings and Pashtuns Don't Say Thank You

Malala was the best student in her class but soon had some competition from a new girl, Malka-e-Noor, who beat her at year's end. Malala got into trouble for stealing, and after this she resolved never to lie or steal again. She also resolved not to wear jewellery...'What are these baubles that tempt me? Why should I lose my character for a few metal trinkets?'

The Pashtuns also thought that a good deed should never be forgotten so there was never any need to say thank you. On the flip side they never forgave or forgot. The 'Pashtunwali' code of revenge was strong and had no limits, which is why longstanding feuds arose.

Feuds were common and Malala recounts the story of two families being locked in a dispute over a plot of land in the forest. Three brothers of one family were ambushed and killed in the forest by their uncle and his men. Instead of revenge, Malala's father would mediate in such disputes, arguing that instead of continuing the violence, people should just get on with their lives. We are also told how the politicians stole from the people they were supposed to represent.

Malala had been born in the brief time Pakistan 'was sort of democratic' but General Musharraf had organised a coup, thrown the elected Prime Minister, Navaz Sharif, into prison, and then exiled him. The General promised much to the people and delivered little. The Deputy Commissioners they sent to Swat to rule were either incompetent or corrupt or both.

Malala had three good friends and one, Moniba, wanted to do well at school and avoid trouble so her brothers didn't stop her going. Both she and Malala entered a public speaking contest which Moniba won because her speech was more emotive than the one Malala's father wrote for her. After this Malala wrote her own speeches and delivered them 'from my heart'.

6. Children of the Rubbish Mountain

Malala's family had a better life economically and they now had a TV. Malala had to go to the tip one day to dispose of the family rubbish and here she saw real poverty with the children sorting rubbish. Malala's family also had people staying in their house who had suffered extreme poverty and Malala's father often gave free places in his school to the needy. This caused problems as the social divisions in society were strong.

Her father's work to help others made him a 'well-known figure' and people listened to him. He didn't like corruption and was a leader in organising people to engage in 'local concerns'. He also wrote poetry which made him popular. He was absent from home frequently because of this and 9/11 had made everything more complex. America was after the terrorist Osama bin Laden and this made Musharraf popular in the West despite the fact that Pakistan's Intelligence Service had 'created the Taliban'.

Muslim feeling was mixed and some saw bin Laden as a 'hero' and conspiracy theories were rampant. Musharraf said that Pakistan would co-operate with America. Maulana Sufi Mohammed issued a fatwa against the U.S. and thousands died. Their wives and children still waited for them as there was no proof of death. Bin Laden and his men escaped to Swat taking advantage of *Pashtunwali* hospitality'. American money never reached the people.

Through all this, Malala became interested in politics and tried to help local people. She prayed a lot for them.

7. The *Mufti* Who Tried to Close Our School

A *mufti* is an 'Islamic scholar and authority on Islamic law' but as Malala's father points out, in reality anyone could call themselves that. A mufti called Ghulamullah tried to shut the school down because girls were attending. He first tried to bribe the owner of the school building but was refused. Malala points out that there were two main streams of Islam and Pakistan was created for Muslims although there were also some Christians and Ahmadiis.

The founder of Pakistan, Muhammad Ali Jinnah, wanted 'a land of tolerance'. A few days before Pakistan's independence he gave a famous speech: 'You may belong to any religion or caste- that has nothing to do with the business of the state.' He thought the business of the state was separate to religion but died before his dream could be realised. Muslims are 'split between Sunnis and Shias'. Malala discussed their differences.

The mufti continued his campaign forming a delegation that came to Malala's home but her father won the argument and the school continued. Ghulamullah was also causing trouble in his own family as well. General Musharraf had a policy of 'enlightened moderation' and women had some increased freedom, even in law but these never applied in Malala's Pashtun homeland where religion held sway. It was a very conservative area and militants wanted a 'morality police' like the Afghan Taliban had set up.

The mufti became bolder in the changing political climate and again tried to stop the school and especially the girls attending, but he failed. Things throughout the valley became more difficult as the war got closer and some al-Qaeda leaders were allegedly hiding in Pakistan. The Pakistan secret police had close links to them. The U.S. began drone attacks against key militants in

Pakistan and this caused further angst and created more militancy amongst local tribes. No one in the town would listen to Malala's father when he warned them about the increasing militancy.

8. The Autumn of the Earthquake

In October 2005, a huge earthquake of '7.6 on the Richter Scale' devastated Pakistan killing 73,000 people and displacing 3.5 million. Everyone rallied together to help the worst affected areas. Everyone was worried about relatives and while the government and American troops assisted in the recovery, some Muslim welfare groups who provided assistance were infiltrated by Islamic militants so they could get into the area. They used religion to rally people and some of the money raised from British Pakistanis was diverted to terrorism rather than relief.

The earthquake orphaned 11,000 children. In the remote areas much of the relief was provided by volunteers from Islamic charities, some of whom were fronts for militant groups such as Jamaat-ul-Dawa(JuD) the welfare wing of Lashkar-e-Taiba(LeT). This organisation had been established to encourage military action to annex Kashmir from India. JuD offered orphan boys free food and lodging in a JuD madras (school). They were engaged in an educational curriculum which involved learning the Quran by heart, but that did not include science or literature. JuD's intentions included training the orphans for *jihad* purposes. The militants said the earthquake was a warning from God about 'women's freedom and obscenity' and they demanded sharia law.

Plot Questions and Activities for Part One of *I Am Malala*

- What does the Preface to this edition offer the reader?
- Why does Malala begin with her shooting? How does this position the reader? What might be extraordinary about her experiences?
- Describe why a girl baby isn't celebrated in Pakistan.
- Discuss Malala's early family life.
- Analyse with specific quotes for, why 'a program of Islamisation' under General Zia changed the way women were treated in Pakistan.
- In two paragraphs, state why Malala's father doesn't want to be known as the falcon.
- What does Benazir Bhutto bring to Pakistan?
- Why is 9/11 a catastrophic incident for Malala's valley? If you don't know about 9/11 try these sites:
  - *https://en.wikipedia.org/wiki/September_11_attacks*
  - *http://www.history.com/topics/9-11-attacks*
- Describe village life in Pakistan. Why might it be boring for the older children?
- Why does Malala not wear earrings?
- What impact do the children of the rubbish mountain have on Malala?
- Discuss why Muslims might have conflicting feelings about Osama bin Laden?
- What is a *mufti*?
- Summarise the founding of Pakistan as described by Malala in Chapter 7.
- What is General Musharraf's policy of 'enlightened moderation'?
- Why are the Taliban opposed to girls' schooling?
- Do you think the experiences Malala has growing up are unique or is it her attitude to them? Or both?
- Research the Pashtun people. Why are they so conservative?
- Describe the impact of the earthquake.
- What is '*jihad*'?
- What is the symbolic purpose of the earthquake to the Taliban? Discuss how they twist it for religious purposes to increase their power.

PART TWO: THE VALLEY OF DEATH

9. Radio Mullah

Malala was ten years old when 'the Taliban' came. They were heavily armed and 'strange-looking' and they wore badges with 'SHARIA LAW OR MARTYRDOM'. The leader Maulana Fazlullah was a pulley chair operator who began as an 'Islamic reformer' and his radio station Mullah FM was used to propagandise the people. They started off 'wisely', encouraging people to abandon bad habits. Initially the reaction from the people was positive and many got rid of their 'TVs, DVDs and CDs'. Only Taliban songs were acceptable.

Malala's father became depressed as people followed this 'high school dropout', Fazullah. Fazlullah then began to attack the government and the khans. He was especially against women as well as music, movies and dancing. This wasn't part of the Holy Quran but many of the poor people listened to his words.

The leader of the Taliban, Sufi Mohammad, then began to attack girls' education and schools. The Taliban passed edict after edict restricting life, especially for women, even banning shopping. They instituted their own courts, stopped vaccinations and began to get more aggressive using suicide bombers and murder. The Taliban even put a note on the school gate. Malala's father responded in a letter to the newspaper saying they prayed to the same God.

10. Toffees, Tennis Balls and the Buddhas of Swat

Malala begins 'First the Taliban took our music, then our Buddhas, then our history' (p102). Swat is a wonderful place but the Taliban destroyed everything, even the ancient Buddha statues. They stole the resources and banned 'anything'. They began to murder the police and bully the people and nobody did anything about it. Their propaganda was strong and they burned TVs and computers.

The Taliban had even gone into Islamabad to enforce their views. People began to worry that 'the militants could take over the capital'. The military finally moved on them and surrounded the most troublesome 'Red Mosque' where two brothers Abdul Aziz and Abdul Rashid ran a terror cell. Abdul Aziz escaped by dressing as a woman in a burqa. The military won a bloody battle but the Taliban then declared war on the government.

Hostilities became worse but there was hope when Benazir Bhutto returned from exile, a move which the Americans helped to broker. This brought great hope for democracy and huge crowds came out to greet her. The fighting increased from the Taliban and they began to butcher and humiliate people. Eventually Benazir Bhutto was assassinated by the Taliban and all hope was lost for the country.

11. The Clever Class

School kept Malala going even though school uniforms and equipment had to be hidden. The competition at school was strong and Malka-e-Noor continued to excel. At the end of 2007 the army hadn't 'got rid of the Taliban' despite a heavy presence in the area. The school was a 'haven' and kept Malala going in the dark days. Other girls dropped out, especially when the Taliban began blowing schools up. At one bombing of a funeral, fifty-five people were killed.

At one point in 2008 the elders created an assembly to challenge Fazlullah and the Taliban. They began to question the Taliban leaders and used media to say the Taliban were not about Islam. They said 'Don't support Talibanisation, it's inhuman' and encouraged people to speak out. Malala's father and his activist friends and then Malala and her friends began to give interviews and journalists were generally sympathetic. Despite this, schools kept being destroyed and then looted (about 400 by the end of 2008).

Many of these students transferred to Malala's school and brought even more competition. A new government under Asif Zardari didn't change anything but in Swat it was still safer than in the surrounding countryside. During Ramadan the Taliban destroyed the power and gas utilities. No clean water meant cholera developed. In 2008, the Taliban announced that all girls' schools would close. Malala's father never suggested that Malala should withdraw from school.

12. The Bloody Square

The Taliban would dump bodies in the square as a warning. One night a woman, Shabana, was murdered for being a dancer. Dancing was considered immoral by the Taliban and women would be killed if they danced. Musicians even stopped playing. Malala points out what made the Taliban popular:

> 'Manual workers made a great contribution to our society but received no recognition, and this is the reason so

many of them joined the Taliban – to finally achieve status and power.' (p124)

The Taliban infiltrated Swat and every aspect of society. They stole for weapons and many wealthier people fled. There was no protection for ordinary people and Malala's family came under threat. Her father slept away from the house and death was everywhere. The war was close and the government was helpless, terror 'had made people cruel' and the 'the Taliban bulldozed both our Pashtun values and the values of Islam' (p128).

13. The Diary of Gul Makai

Malala was asked to write a diary about life under the Taliban by the BBC. She began this with the journalist Abdul Hai Kakar, and her blog appeared in Urdu on the BBC website. Malala wrote anonymously using a pseudonym 'Gul Makai', the name of a heroine in a Pashtun folk tale. Malala wrote about the violence, school, the burqa and other aspects of life. It was dangerous and there was murder and violence all around the town. The diary received significant attention :

'I began to see that the pen and the words that came from it can be much more powerful than machine guns, tanks or helicopters. We were learning how to struggle. We were learning how powerful we are when we speak.' (p131)

Malala's class went from 27 to 10 members and the Taliban began to destroy all forms of education. Finally Malala's school was closed and Malala appeared in a New York Times website documentary about it. In the documentary Malala pleaded to the world to 'save our school, save our Pakistan, save our Swat'.

The Taliban hated education because they thought it 'Westernised' people. Malala responded that 'Education is education. We should learn everything and then choose which path to follow. Education is neither Eastern nor Western, it is human.' (p135)

Adam, the journalist from the *New York Times,* took Malala and her family to Islamabad for a break. Even in the capital there were terror attacks. The family returned to the realities of Swat – their home which they were not ready to leave.

14. A Funny Kind of Peace

Eventually the pressure mounted on the Taliban and they allowed girls' education up to Year 4. The girls went to school, including Malala who was in year 5. This is one secret that Malala didn't share on her blog. In 2009 the provincial government and the Taliban struck a peace deal. In exchange for introducing sharia law in Swat, the Taliban agreed to stop fighting.

Unfortunately the violence soon resumed and it became clear that the peace deal was a 'mirage'. The Americans were also unhappy with the government for caving in to the terrorists. The Taliban were now 'even more barbaric' and patrolled the streets looking to commit acts of violence including flogging women. The army appeared to be enabling Taliban leaders and at a peace assembly, Sufi Mohammad appeared to threaten the whole country, saying that they were coming to attack Islamabad. People were disappointed and the Taliban spread to Buner, destroying normal life in that area, including closing a Muslim shrine. Finally the army acted to drive out the Taliban and the residents of Swat were told to leave.

15 Leaving the Valley

Malala had to leave Swat and this was the hardest thing in her life to date. She bemoaned the fact that Swat may never be free. She and her family became IDPs (internally displaced persons) and drove off with few possessions on the crowded roads to Mardam. Pashtun hospitality came to the fore and they all found places to sleep. They kept journeying and eventually reached Karshat, her mother's village.

They followed the fighting on the radio and tried to keep in contact with their father. Finally he called them to Peshawar and from there they went to Islamabad. Here they met the American Ambassador Richard Holbrooke and Malala did a radio interview. They then moved to Haripur and here Malala had her twelfth birthday. In the upheaval, nobody remembered.

Plot Questions and Activities for Part Two of *I Am Malala*

- Discuss the impact of the Taliban on everyday life for the people of Swat.
- Why did the Taliban hate education? Could this hatred be part of their own insecurities as many were illiterate?
- Describe why the Taliban destroyed the ancient Buddhas of Swat.
- Discuss how Malala's family life changed over the course of Part Two of the text.
- Analyse the impact of the 'Red Mosque' incident in Islamabad.
- How did the death of Benazir Bhutto destroy the hope of the people?
- Why was the army ineffective against the Taliban?
- What impact did sharia law have on the general population? To learn more about sharia law you can visit these sites.
  - *https://en.wikipedia.org/wiki/Sharia*
  - *http://www.theaustralian.com.au/news/nation/what-exactly-is-sharia-law/news-story/4e3c627f248841b46d465b4c79dec59a*
  - *http://www.sbs.com.au/news/article/2014/09/23/explainer-what-sharia-law*
- Discuss the effect of the Taliban blowing schools up.
- Why was Shabana murdered?
- Discuss why Malala wrote that the values of Pashtun and Islam had been destroyed at the conclusion of 'The Bloody Square'.
- What is a pseudonym?
- How did Malala come to write for the BBC?
- How did the Taliban complicate life for Malala specifically during this period?
- Discuss the impact of the video of the Taliban flogging a girl.
- Why do you think the Taliban didn't want peace? Why did Sufi Mohammad encourage more violence?
- Describe Malala's family journey all the way to Haripur.
- How do you perceive Malala at this point in the text?

PART THREE: THREE GIRLS, THREE BULLETS

16. The Valley of Sorrows

The return to Swat was not a happy one as the area was under the complete control of the military but at least the Taliban were gone. Fortunately, Malala's family's home had not been looted and the school was still intact. The soldiers had been living there in the school buildings and the family found a note in which the army blamed the locals for allowing the Taliban to control the area. Many people were arrested and sent to camps to de-radicalise them. Fazlullah the Taliban leader had escaped and only two Taliban leaders had been captured.

School began on August 1 and the main topic was the trip to Islamabad for the girls arranged by Shiza Shahid who had now finished her studies at Stanford. They had workshops on how to help get over the trauma of living under the Taliban. They learnt to speak out and tell their stories. The group also enjoyed some fun activities like listening to music, sightseeing, going to the theatre and art. They met women who were educated (eg lawyers, doctors and activists) who had important jobs but also kept their culture and traditions. They even saw women with their heads completely uncovered. The students went to Army Headquarters and met Major General Athar Abbas who briefed them and invited questions. The girls asked lots of questions and told him they wanted the Taliban brought to justice. They gave speeches at the Islamabad Club which made people cry.

Malala's father still had problems as he still had to pay the teachers despite the school being closed. They wrote to the General they had met in Islamabad and he sent them the money to pay the staff. The family kept giving interviews. They were very unhappy that the Taliban leaders were not captured as the suicide bombings continued. Malala was elected speaker of the District Child Assembly in Swat which passed resolutions, calling for an end to child labour, asking for reconstruction of all schools and other matters. Some of these resolutions were acted on.

Malala came first at school and life was returning to some sort of normality but in July 2010 the school was flooded and the whole of Pakistan was affected. The power was gone and many houses were destroyed, villages were washed away, the harvests destroyed and there was no clean water. Again some Islamic groups used this as a warning about turning from God, for the music and dancing enjoyed at recent festivals. The Americans helped in the rescue and rebuilding but President Zardari continued his European travel. Aid organisations were threatened by the Taliban and this didn't help efforts. They used the flood to resume their terror and began to murder again.

17. Praying to Be Tall

Malala 'stopped growing' at thirteen and wanted to be taller so she could sound more authoritive. One of the girls in her class was married off as she reached puberty. The army had a few side businesses and one was a TV show called '*Beyond the Call of Duty*' which was about their heroic battles in Swat with the Taliban. There were many missing men because of the fighting and all over Pakistan women were in limbo and there was no official help for them. Malala's father was involved with helping some.

A major incident at the time was the blasphemy trial of a Christian woman who was accused and sentenced to death. This caused world-wide outrage and one man in Pakistan who spoke out against it was Salman Taseer, the Governor of Punjab, who was then murdered by one of his bodyguards. Many even praised the murderer. Malala's father also came under threat. It was usually India that got the blame for everything that went wrong in Pakistan but now it was America as a CIA agent had killed two Pakistanis who were trying to rob him. It blew up into an international incident but the Americans continued their drone attacks anyway.

Next, Osama bin Laden was found and killed by the Americans and they learnt he had been hiding less than a mile from the military academy. Malala's father wondered why the army couldn't catch a terrorist on their doorstep. Feelings in Pakistan were mixed and some felt the army had failed and others felt Pakistan had been humiliated because the US acted alone in their attack on bin Laden.

In 2011 Malala was nominated for a peace prize and was invited to speak at an education gala. She then won Pakistan's first peace prize and got to meet the Prime Minister. Malala returned to school and things were going well. The family had some money and Malala vowed to continue to fight for education.

18. The Woman and the Sea

Malala was astonished that her aunt had never seen the sea despite living close by. Her husband wouldn't take her and she couldn't read signs to get there herself. Malala thought of other lands where women were free whereas in Pakistan they couldn't make any decisions for themselves but this restriction wasn't written anywhere in the Quran. Malala flew to Karachi in a plane with her parents for the first time to speak at the opening of a school named after her. Karachi had a high level of violence because it had divisions between the Pashtun and the *mohajirs* (mohajir people). Here they visited museums and the Mohammad Ali Jinnah memorial. Malala thought the country would be better off thinking about practical issues instead of fighting.

A journalist then warned Malala that the Taliban wanted to execute her for advocating 'secularism'. Her family were nervous about returning to Swat but felt they must continue their work. The army said she would be safe in Swat if she kept a low profile.

The regional KPK (Khyber Pakhtunkhwa) government offered to make Malala a peace ambassador, but her father suggested that she should refuse.

19. A Private Talibanisation

The 'private Talibanisation' was about the Taliban now concentrating on those who spoke out against them. The attacks were against peace-builders and civilians but not the army or the police.

Malala's school went on an excursion and afterwards, the Taliban wrote a propaganda letter which they distributed widely. The letter made untrue allegations about the girls (eg vulgarity, obscenity). The family were pressured by the Taliban and the army and then on Malala's fifteenth birthday a peace committee member was murdered. One of Ziauddin's friends (Zahid Khan) was shot in the face and he went to visit the man in hospital. Malala's father was the next target, so he changed his routine but continued to be an activist. The final section of the chapter is about Malala being 'hassled by a boy':

'Sometimes I think it's easier to be a Twilight vampire than a girl in Swat', I sighed. But really I wished that being hassled by a boy was my biggest problem. (p197)

20. Who Is Malala?

Malala took precautions for her safety and prayed a lot, especially around exam time. She recounted her morning and how her exams were progressing. She stayed late at school and waited for the bus. On the way home it was stopped by two men who ask 'Who is Malala?'

> I didn't get a chance to answer their question … or I would have explained to them why they should let us girls go to school as well as their own sisters and daughters. (p203)

The man then fired three bullets.

Plot Questions and Activities for Part Three of *I Am Malala*

- Discuss how Swat has changed in the family's absence.
- Analyse why the soldiers might blame the people for the Taliban.
- Describe why prisoners were sent to camps to be de-radicalised.
- How does Shiza Shahid help the girls?
- Analyse the impact of positive role models for the girls.
- Discuss the meeting with Major General Athar Abbas.
- How does Malala's father manage to pay his staff?
- What impact does the flood have on Pakistan as a whole and Swat in particular?
- Discuss why the Taliban might threaten aid agencies trying to help the people of Pakistan.
- Why does Malala wish to be taller?
- What is *'Beyond the Call of Duty'*?
- Analyse why the blasphemy trial was such an important issue around the world.
- Why might the CIA agent killing two robbers create an international incident? What does this say about the mood in Pakistan at the time?
- Who was Osama bin Laden? Why was his death significant in terms of Pakistani-American relations?
- Why does Malala's aunt make her think about the role of women in Pakistani society?
- Discuss how violence is a part of life in Pakistan.
- What is 'secularism'?
- How do the Taliban put pressure on Malala and her family?
- Describe the day of the shooting.

PART FOUR: BETWEEN LIFE AND DEATH

21. 'God, I entrust her to you'

The bus driver took Malala straight to the hospital and the news that she had been shot spread fast. Her father completed his speech and rushed to the hospital. Later they learnt that the bullet had missed Malala's brain and that two other girls had also been shot. The army took Malala by helicopter to Peshawar where she was taken to the Combined Military Hospital. Here they discovered that the injury was more serious than the initial scans showed.

Visitors came from all over Pakistan, including dignitaries. Malala's brain was swelling because of bone splinters and she needed an operation of great complexity. The neurosurgeon, Colonel Junaid, decided she needed the operation immediately. It was a five hour operation and Malala survived. The Taliban claimed responsibility for her shooting, branding her 'pro-West' and 'preaching secularism'.

After the operation, the army chief, General Kayani visited. He arranged for two British doctors to see Malala. They were fortunately in Pakistan assisting the army set up a hospital. Dr Fiona Reynolds was not happy with Malala's care but thought that the girl was 'salvageable'. The Interior Minister brought Malala a passport as many people were calling for her to be taken overseas.

22. Journey into the Unknown

Malala's father thought she would die after two days as the hospital didn't make the changes to her treatment as recommended by Dr Reynolds. Fortunately the doctor was still in Pakistan with two nurses and they came to help. Malala was then flown to Rawalpindi under Dr Reynolds' care and by now the doctor had realised Malala's importance. Malala and her family and carers were all under threat from the Taliban but international pressure was growing because of the shooting. Some radicals spoke out against Malala but offers of help from across the world flowed in.

The British offered to treat Malala at the Queen Elizabeth Hospital in Birmingham and arrangements were made. It was a major logistical exercise. Eventually due to political concerns the ruling family of the United Arab Emirates offered their private jet which had a hospital on-board. Unfortunately Malala's family didn't have the documentation to travel and Malala's father refused to leave his wife and sons so Dr Fiona was given *loco parentis* to take her. They arrived in Birmingham safely while her parents waited back in Pakistan.

Plot Questions and Activities for Part Four of *I Am Malala*

- Why were the bus driver's actions important?
- Analyse why the army might wish to be involved in her recovery.
- Why is the arrival of Dr Fiona vital for Malala?
- Why is this experience so emotive and extreme for Malala's parents and family?
- Think about the interest in Malala and her injury. Why might this be a huge political issue in Pakistan?
- Comment on how human experiences can be impacted by external forces.

PART FIVE: A SECOND LIFE

23. 'The Girl Shot in the Head, Birmingham'

Malala woke up a week after the shooting and she was disoriented but reassured by a Muslim chaplain. Malala found it difficult to think as her head ached and everything was mixed up in her mind. One of her ears kept bleeding and the left side of her face wasn't working properly. Dr Fiona gave her a white teddy bear that she named Lily.

Malala had two main concerns, her father and the cost of the treatment. She was reassured on both issues. When she was up to it, the doctors allowed her to call her parents who told her they would be there soon.

Malala's father was angry because the army had earlier told him Malala would be safe but now they admitted they were searching for a gang of Taliban who they knew had been there all along (and also killed his friend Zahid Khan).

Malala slowly began to piece the story of her shooting together and recalled some images of the incident. As she recovered she wanted more details and Rehanna, the Muslim chaplain, talked to her about the shooting from a Muslim perspective. Her family were moved from the army hostel to Islamabad. Later they learnt it was the civilian government that was holding things up for political purposes, including a fear that the family would embarrass them by claiming asylum. Eventually Malala's parents arrived in Birmingham after ten days.

The nursing staff were very good to Malala and bought her clothes and sourced halal food for her. They brought her movies and helped with her physiotherapy. Malala met the hospital press officer, another Fiona, who tells her of the world-wide interest in her story. Everyone wanted to see her and she received over 8,000 cards, presents and prayers. She thought that the Taliban had made her campaign global. At this point Malala didn't realise she wouldn't be going home.

24. 'They have snatched her smile'

Malala was moved from intensive care and could look out the window to see England for the first time. When her family arrived, they wept and Malala thought that her parents looked older. Malala's facial nerve was damaged and her parents were upset that the Taliban 'have snatched her smile'. Malala was denied visitors to aid her rehabilitation but several important people were briefed on her condition.

The family learnt that a *talib* called Ataullah Khan had been identified as her attacker. They doubted he would be caught as the only arrests made were the bus driver and the school accountant – both innocent men.

The United Nations designated 10 November as Malala Day. Malala prepared for the big operation on her facial nerve which went well. Her headaches started to ease and she began to read again. By 6 December she had recovered enough to have a trip out of the hospital to Birmingham Botanical Gardens. Two days later President Zardari called on her and it caused a media frenzy. The President offered her father a job and a diplomatic passport so that he wouldn't have to leave Britain.

In 2013 the family had their own apartment in Birmingham and Malala soon realised that life here was very different to Swat. Women were free and this was so new to the family. Malala skyped her friends at school who missed the competition she provided. Malala still had to have her skull surgery and rather than use her own bone they substituted a titanium one. She also received a cochlear implant.

She praised God for her survival and life and the readers learnt that her two friends who were shot had also come to the UK to continue their education.

EPILOGUE

One Child, One Teacher, One Book, One Pen...
Birmingham, August 2013

The family now had a rented house that felt 'big and empty' , 'like a luxury house arrest'. It was very different to Swat and lonely compared to their old house which was always full of people:

> We are just a wall's distance from the next house but it feels miles away. p256

Now they had all that they needed but had also lost much, especially Malala's father. He had to leave behind the school which he had built up over twenty years to 1100 students and 70 teachers. He was now known as Malala's father rather than Malala being known as his daughter.

Malala went to school in Birmingham and was a little lonely, missing her friends back in Swat. She told Moniba on skype about the women with jobs 'we couldn't imagine in Swat'. Malala could remember bits of the shooting and she still worried about her security. At the time of the Epilogue, Malala had been nominated for the Nobel Peace Prize (and in 2014 she was awarded it along with Kailash Satyarthi, an Indian activist).

Malala spoke at the United Nations in New York about providing free education to every child in the world and received a standing ovation.

Ironically Malala had received wide support internationally but was most harshly criticised from people within her own country of Pakistan. She received a letter from a Taliban commander but refused to answer as they didn't rule the country. Malala wanted to go back to Pakistan one day but her father worried and made 'excuses'.

Malala wants to see education for every boy and every girl in the world:

> I love my God. I thank my Allah ... By giving me this height to reach people, he has also given me great responsibilities. Peace in every home, every street, every village, every country - this is my dream. Education for every boy and every girl in the world....

Malala finished the Epilogue with the line:

> 'I am Malala. My world has changed but I have not.'

ADDITIONAL TEXTUAL MATERIAL

The end of the text contains a glossary, mainly of Pakistani terminology, an acknowledgements section, a timeline of important events in Pakistani and Swat history and an interview with her U.S. editor, Judy Clan. It covers her current life and thoughts for the future.

Plot Questions and Activities for Part Five and Epilogue of *I Am Malala*

- What were Malala's main concerns when she woke up?
- Who is Rehanna and how did she help Malala?
- Why was the arrival of her parents from Pakistan a defining moment for Malala?
- Discuss why the family had little faith that the gunman would be caught. Is this a realistic or pessimistic view? Explain.
- Describe life in England for Malala's family?
- Comment on Malala's final thought,

> 'I am Malala. My world has changed but I have not.'

in terms of human experiences.

SETTING

The setting of the text is mainly the Swat district of the Khyber Pakhtunkhwa province in Pakistan. The final few chapters are set in Birmingham, England. Pakistan is a place that Malala says is, 'centuries behind this one' (p1) when she is in England. The map here gives you some idea of the look and shape of Pakistan and includes some of the cities mentioned in the text.

Malala revered her Pakistani heritage and states,

> 'But when you are exiled from your homeland, where your fathers and forefathers were born and where you have centuries of history, it's very painful. You can no longer touch the soil or hear the sweet sound of the rivers. Fancy hotels and meetings in palaces cannot replace the sense of home.' (pxx)

We also see this has an impact on her family as her mother is in Birmingham 'but mentally she's in Swat – her homesickness is horrible'. (pxx)

Malala often called her homeland 'beloved' and missed the structures and people the family had around them despite their humble house and existence. Malala also wrote about the beauty of the region,

> 'We lived in the most beautiful place in all the world. My valley, the Swat Valley, is a heavenly kingdom of mountains, gushing waterfalls and crystal-clear lakes. WELCOME TO PARADISE, it says on a sign as you enter the valley. In olden times Swat was called Uddyana, which means 'garden'. We have fields of wild flowers, orchards of delicious fruit, emerald mines and rivers full of trout.' (p11)

We also have the contrasting realities of living in the region and in Pakistan in general. The radical Islamic violence is clearly demonstrated with Malala's shooting but this, in fact, is one of the minor acts of violence in a society that has it as a way of life. We see endemic Taliban violence through their extreme religious views which gives them an excuse to brutalise whole populations, destroy history and extort from the local peoples. We also read of systemic corruption in politics and in the bureaucracy and some of the poor living conditions in the country.

These are the contrasts of Pakistan and we also read of the kind heartedness of many of the people and the goodwill of many towards Malala's cause and the well-being of people in general. The Pashtun hospitality is particularly cited as an example of this. It is a complex country with complex problems and this becomes clear as we read. The physical issues also become a significant part of the experience of living in Pakistan and we read of two major ones in the text – the earthquake and the flood. Both cause massive infrastructure issues and a tragic loss of life.

It is easy to see here that setting impacts greatly on human experiences and it is influential on how people live.

Setting Questions and Activities

- What role does Swat play in the development of Malala's early experiences? What type of place is Swat in terms of landscape? Can you see why Malala might be attached to the area?
- Research the Pashtun people. What general qualities do they have that make living a very social experience for the community?
- How did Malala handle her visits to the cities such as Islamabad and Karachi? What differences did she notice and how do you see the cities?
- Discuss the impact of the Taliban on Swat.
- On the Internet run a search for either the massive earthquake of 2005 or the flooding of 2010 which inundated Pakistan. Look at the information on the social dislocation. How did Malala use this to show how the Taliban and other radical Islamic groups infiltrate areas and begin to propagandise and radicalise people?
- Describe how Malala saw life in Birmingham. It should be 500 words outlining the problems and positives in her life.

CHARACTER ANALYSIS

Malala

Malala is an inspirational young woman and her memoir highlights several key aspects of her character.

Malala has a questioning mind which is strongly attuned to the social realities of her region, especially the treatment of women in society. While she lives in a society where women's freedom is severely restricted, her own experience is filled with opportunities as her father does not wish Malala to be limited in the same way:

> My father always said, 'Malala will be free as a bird' (p20)

> My father used to say, 'I will protect your freedom, Malala. Carry on with your dreams.' (p55)

> The media needs interviews. They want to interview a small girl, but the girls are scared, and even if they're not, their parents won't allow it. I have a father who isn't scared, who stands by me. He said, 'You are a child and it's your right to speak.' (p117)

From the outset, it is clear that Malala is compassionate and sensitive to the needs of others. She is deeply moved by the plight of children living close by to her on the rubbish dump at a young age (see Chapter 6) and as she matures, this develops into a strong resolve to bring practical help to children like them:

> I saw a young girl selling oranges. She was scratching marks on a scrap of paper with a nail to account for the oranges she had sold as she could not read or write.

I vowed to do everything in my power to help educate girls just like her. This was the war I was going to fight. (pp 81–82)

Malala is named after Malalai of Maiwand, the 'greatest heroine of Afghanistan' (p9). Malalai inspired the Afghan army to defeat the British in the Second Anglo-Afghan War and died in the battle.

Malala is passionate about school and education. She loved learning and going to school and it was a 'haven' for Malala during the dark days.

Malala wrote an anonymous diary for the BBC about life under the Taliban. It was known as the Diary of Gul Makai (see chapter 13). Through the experience of writing the diary and seeing it receive attention beyond the BBC, Malala began to learn how influential this could be:

I began to see that the pen and the words that come from it can be much more powerful than machine guns, tanks or helicopters. We were learning how to struggle. And we were learning how powerful we are when we speak. (p131)

Malala has a strong inner voice and sense of her future vocation. When Malala heard about the assassination of Benazir Bhutto, her heart said to her:

Why don't you go there and fight for women's rights? (p111)

In the face of the Taliban threat, Malala wrote:

In my heart was the belief that God would protect me. If I am speaking for my rights, for the rights of girls, I am not doing anything wrong.... There is a saying in the Quran, The falsehood has to go and the truth will prevail.'

> *If one man, Fazlullah, can destroy almost everything, why can't one girl change it?* I wondered. I prayed to God every night to give me strength. (p117)

As her profile grew, Malala received a number of awards and realised that she could make a difference. When Malala won the first National Peace Prize, the Prime Minister of Pakistan presented the award to her and she presented him with a long list of demands:

> I knew he would not take my demands seriously so I didn't push very hard. I thought, One day I will be a politician and do these things myself.

Malala is at the beginning of her adult life when the memoir concludes. With such a large amount achieved in her teens, much more is expected of the years ahead and she is determined to continue her quest:

> I know God stopped me from going to the grave ... People prayed to God to spare me, and I was spared for a reason – to use my life for helping people... p255

The link below is a recent interview with Malala, aged 20 at the time of commencing her world tour to visit girls and support their aims and education:

https://www.thelily.com/our-qa-with-malala-yousafzai-nobel-peace-prize-winner-and-education-advocate/

Ziauddin

I am Malala makes it clear that Ziauddin has played a very strong role in nurturing and shaping Malala to be who she is.

Ziauddin is a very principled and courageous person who cares deeply about his family and is not afraid to speak out against the authorities. He is not limited by the perspectives of others but always thinks things through for himself.

Malala recounts how her father added her name to the family tree which previously showed only male relatives: 'My father, Ziauddin, is different from most Pashtun men.'

Ziauddin named Malala after the well known Afghan heroine and throughout her life he encouraged her to be brave and principled and to stand up for what is right.

> He came from humble beginnings but through education and 'force of personality he made a good living for us and a name for himself.' p17

Ziauddin became involved in politics at university and was a very engaged citizen in peace-building efforts and in his leadership of the local association of private schools.

Chapter 2 helps the reader understand the formation of Ziauddin's character. While always striving to please his father, he overcame his stutter through courageously entering a public speaking competition. He was pleased to earn his father's admiration and to be called a 'falcon' until he realised that although the falcon flies high, it is a cruel bird.

At every stage throughout the memoir, Ziauddin encourages his daughter not to be limited by society, and to take opportunities given to her:

> My father used to say, 'I will protect your freedom, Malala. Carry on with your dreams.'

His own character is well developed through the memoir through his struggles and high level of engagement in local events and issues. Ziauddin is involved in the establishment of the Global Peace Council in Swat to preserve the environment of Swat and to promote peace and education among local people.

Malala often provides Ziauddin's perspective on issues she recounts and from this we learn that he has a strong sense of justice and compassion. He views education as the key to solving Pakistan's problems and does all he can to educate people in his own school, to foster the value of education in wider society and to provide practical help to those who need it.

Ziauddin is an influential person in Swat:

> Even though he was not a khan or a rich man, people listened to him. They knew he would have something interesting to say at workshops and seminars and wasn't afraid to criticise the authorities ... (p68)

Later, when the Taliban leave a threatening note on the school's gate, Ziauddin responds with a reply in the newspaper, pointing out that they all worship the same God. He continues to give media interviews throughout the terrifying days of the Taliban, and resolves to tell the truth in the face of violence and repression.

The relationship between Malala and her father is especially close:

All children are special to their parents, but to my father I was his universe. I had been his comrade in arms for so long, first secretly as Gul Makai, then quite openly as Malala. (p208)

When the family live in Birmingham after Malala was shot, Malala recounts:

All he worked for for over almost twenty years has been left behind: the school he built up from nothing, which now has three buildings with 1,100 pupils and seventy teachers. I know he felt proud at what he had created, a poor boy from that narrow village between the Black and White Mountains. (p258)

In Swat he had achieved respect and status in society through his activities and the help he gave people. (p258)

Malala gives credit to Ziauddin throughout the memoir for encouraging her at all times and never allowing her to be limited by anyone.

Toor Pekai – Malala's mother

There is not nearly as much attention given to Malala's mother in the memoir but she is very much appreciated by Malala and is a constant and positive force in Malala's life. In Malala's early years her mother took a larger responsibility because Ziauddin was often absent with his activist engagements.

Toor is also a strong woman and although she has grown up in a more traditional family, not attending school for long herself, she too values education and is strongly supportive of Malala.

During the hours and days after Malala was shot, her strength and faith came to the fore. While Ziauddin waited anxiously, seeking to bargain with God, Toor interrupted him:

> 'God is not a miser,' she said. 'He will give me back my daughter as she was.' (p215)

> She told my father she felt I would live but he could not see how. (p220)

Maulana Fazlullah and the Taliban

Islamic militants and the Taliban also play a significant role in Malala's memoir. The one who is arguably given the most coverage is Maulana Fazlullah, a 28 year old former pulley chair operator who became the Taliban leader in Swat and who broadcast on the radio known as Mullah FM. Read Chapter 9 for an introduction to Fazlullah.

Fazlullah was 'very wise' initially and introduced himself as an Islamic reformer and interpreter of the Quran, encouraging people to good habits. He was charismatic and while some people talked of him as a great scholar, Malala's father pointed out that he was a high-school dropout who spread ignorance.

Hidayatullah, a friend of Malala's father explained their way of operating:

> They want to win the hearts and minds of the people so they first see what the local problems are and target those responsible, and that way they get the support of the silent majority ... After, when they get power, they behave like the criminals they once hunted down.'

The Swat Taliban did just that. Firstly they collected and burnt music, DVDs and televisions and began to act violently against the government, the army and the police. They restricted the freedom of women, closed beauty parlours and told women not to go to the bazaar to shop. Fazlullah set up a local court to administer speedy justice and punishment. Then he banned vaccinations.

His men patrolled the streets looking for offenders against his decrees.

Fazlullah incited violence and after about a year of Mullah FM, murders of khans and political activists began. The police and army seemed to do nothing about it and the police fled their posts. Flags of the Taliban began appearing on police stations.

It seemed that there were few people willing to stand up to the Taliban:

> All this happened and nobody did a thing. (p103)

Eventually the Pakistan Government sent the army to confront the Taliban (Chapter 10) but there was evidence of collusion between the government and the Taliban and the violence was allowed to continue.

While the Taliban used religion to persuade their followers initially, it was widely recognised that they abused religion for their own purposes. As Malala pointed out:

> They are abusing our religion ... How will you accept Islam if I put a gun to your head and say Islam is the true religion? If they want every person in the world to be Muslim why don't they show themselves to be good Muslims first? (p124)

> Terror had made people cruel. The Taliban bulldozed both our Pashtun values and the values of Islam. p128

A peace deal was struck between the provincial government and the Taliban whereby sharia law was introduced but this was revealed to be a mirage and effectively the Taliban took over (see Chapter 14, A Funny Kind of Peace).

The Pakistan Army eventually drove the Taliban out of Swat, and the residents were told to leave for several months during this time. However even after the civilians were allowed to return, the Taliban crept back and targeted particular opponents (eg those who spoke against them and peace-builders). One of Ziauddin's friends was murdered and Malala and her father became targets. Eventually a member of a Taliban gang shot Malala in the head.

Human Experiences in *I am Malala*

The memoir, *I am Malala* is full of human experiences, both personal and shared. Some of these are life-changing and some are more mundane, everyday experiences.

We need to think through:

- What are some of the key human experiences in the memoir?
- How are these human experiences represented in the text (eg what language techniques, structure, form)?
- What are some of the key ideas flowing from the human experiences and their representation in the text?

What are some of the key human experiences in the memoir?

Some examples might include:

- Growing up in a society where women and girls were discriminated against;
- Life for the Yousafzai family;
- Getting caught stealing from a friend;
- Growing up in Swat under the Taliban;
- Going to school in Mingora;
- Being forced to leave the family home when the area was evacuated;
- The girls' school being closed;
- The girls' trip to Islamabad;
- Speaking out against the Taliban (eg in school, radio and TV interviews, documentaries);
- Life as an internally displaced person / family;
- Malala getting shot on the school bus;
- Life in Birmingham after the shooting.

How are some of the human experiences represented by the text?

Example 1 – Living during the period of the Taliban – use of descriptions, dialogue and contrasting views

Malala gives a detailed eyewitness account that is highly personal and this helps the reader to know her and become familiar with her context. Her tone is conversational. In the first chapter about the Taliban (Radio Mullah), Malala introduces them in the context of what she was reading at the time:

> I was ten when the Taliban came to our valley. Moniba and I had been reading the Twilight books and longed to be vampires. It seemed to us that the Taliban arrived in the night just like Vampires. (p91)

This reminds us of her young age and vulnerability in the face of danger and violence. Malala's account of the Taliban and people's responses to them help the reader understand how they came to be accepted and various perspectives of the time. Her account is very detailed and also personal, including contrasting responses from her own family and the wider community:

> My mother is very devout, and to start with she liked Fazlullah. (p92)

> Sometimes his voice was reasonable, like when adults are trying to persuade you to do something you don't want to, and sometimes it was scary and full of fire. (p92) (Malala, on Fazlullah)

> 'He is just fooling people' (Malala's father) (p93)

> People ... admired his charisma. p93

> 'You must meet Maulana Fazlullah' ... 'He's a great scholar' (p93)

'He's actually a high-school dropout whose real name isn't even Fazlullah' (Malala's father) (p93)

I was confused by Fazlullah's words. In the Holy Quran it is not written that men should go outside and women should work all day in the home. (p95)

Example 2 – Living in the period of the Taliban – represented by contrast

In several places Malala refers to a saying or quote from literature and then finds that she is unable to fit her current experience within its parameters. This technique emphasises that she is living in unique and challenging times. She quotes a favourite line of *The Alchemist* by Paolo Coelho and contrasts it with her own experience:

'When you want something all the universe conspires in helping you achieve it,' it says.

I don't think that Paolo Coelho had come across the Taliban or our useless politicians.

On the day they are forced to leave Swat in 2009, Malala recalls the *tapa* her grandmother used to recite:

'No Pashtun leaves his land of his own sweet will. Either he leaves from poverty or he leaves for love.'

Now we were being driven out for a third reason the *tapa* writer had never imagined – the Taliban.

Example 3 - Living during the period of the Taliban - use of humour

In the highly emotional time when they are required to evacuate their valley, Malala provides a detailed personal description of the day – including her brother's suggestion to put nappies on the chickens so they could bring them (and avoid mess in the car). This moment of humour on a day of devastation underscores the reality of the situation.

She refers back to *Twilight* again in a use of dry humour when a boy shows interest in her:

> 'Sometimes I think it's easier to be a Twilight vampire than a girl in Swat,' I sighed. But really I wished that being hassled by a boy was my biggest problem.

Think about some of the key Human Experiences in *I am Malala* and analyse how these Human Experiences are represented in the text.

Number	Select a key human experience from *I am Malala*	What language techniques are used to represent the human experience? Find quotes to support.
1		
2		
3		

Number	Select a key human experience from *I am Malala*	What language techniques are used to represent the human experience? Find quotes to support.
4		
5		

What are some of the key ideas flowing from the human experiences and their representation in the text?

Some of the key ideas flowing from the human experiences represented in *I am Malala* might be:
- The importance of universal education;
- Leadership – particularly as shown by Malala and her father;
- Courage and Speaking Out in the face of fear;
- Religion and Religious Extremism;
- Gender Equality.

What other key ideas flow from the representation of human experiences in the text?

Select three ideas flowing from the human experiences in the text (use some from above or your own) to unpack in a paragraph below. Find quotes from the text relevant to each key idea.

Key Idea	Quotes

Further Reading:

I Am Malala: A Resource Guide for Educators prepared by the Global Women's Institute at George Washington University (highly recommended):

https://malala.gwu.edu/about-resource-guide-and-toolkit

LANGUAGE TECHNIQUES IN *I AM MALALA*

We have already discussed some of the language techniques of the genre in the introductory notes but this section discusses some of the techniques the author(s) use to engage the reader.

The literary merit of the text is the narrative of events which are significantly interesting to a contemporary audience and the individual qualities Malala possesses. The narrative of events is basically chronological in order based on the life of Malala from birth until she has a new home in Birmingham, England. One of the specific techniques that she uses is anecdote. Many of her stories are told episodically and these anecdotes, especially the personal ones, give us the insights into her character and motivations. These little insights evoke empathy with Malala and her family as they struggle against great odds to advocate for girls' education in Pakistan.

Another technique used in the text is to draw on the cultural history of the Pashtun by re-telling some of the stories and myths, such as the one that surrounds Malala's name and the historical power of that. We also get some brief lessons in the history of the Swat area and Pakistan in general. This makes some of the actions around her more immediate  and contextually understandable. It also provides context for an audience who may have little experience with Pakistan. This also includes much of the reason for the creation of Pakistan, an Islamic state.

Malala's story also uses many terms that are specific to her culture and language(s) and this gives authenticity to the narrative. These terms are usually in italics and there is a glossary at the conclusion of her story to allow the reader to fully understand. These are the only complicated language in the text. It is clearly and simply written and the text is fully accessible to readers of all types and ages.

Another technique used is the inclusion of the colour photographs in two places in the text which allow us insights into Malala's family and the progression of her journey from the first graphic of her as a baby to the final one of her family in Birmingham. These add a touch of authenticity to the narrative, especially the ones of the bus after the shooting and her time in the hospital. It is interesting to put faces to the names in the text.

Questions on Language

- Do you think the story is accessible to the average reader? Support your ideas with evidence from the text.
- List five examples of the use of local dialect and / or words in the text. What is the purpose of including these terms in the text?
- Comment on the use of anecdote in the text. Why is it an effective technique to engage an audience?
- Discuss the use of graphics in the text. Do you think they are helpful in understanding Malala's story?
- Find some examples of the use of myth and legend in the text. Do you think they are used appropriately?
- How realistic do you think the dialogue in the text is? From your understanding, are the reactions to situations believable?

THEMES AND IDEAS

Human Experiences

The human experiences in this text are both individual and collective and clearly show that these experiences range across the whole range of human emotions and qualities – from goodness and caring for others to the evil brutality of the Taliban and much between. We see the fragility of the human experience and the inconsistencies in people's behaviours based on external pressures. Much of this is seen with a real immediacy because of the autobiographical nature of the story. Let's now look explicitly at the examples of human experiences in the text.

One of the critical human experiences in the text is the shooting of Malala which catapulted her to international fame. The concept of being shot for wanting to go to school is alien to our culture and certainly drew much interest from the rest of the world. Malala challenged the assumptions and way the radical Islamist Taliban saw the world. Through their blinkered vision of what the world should be, the Taliban wished to make it inconsistent with common humanity and would go to any lengths of brutality and cruelty to make reality reflect their dream. Malala's personal example and aptitude for speaking the truth made her a threat to them and they took the abominable act of trying to murder her to stop her. Ironically, as she points out, it only strengthened her cause and made it a world-wide phenomenon.

Malala's shooting was an extreme individual experience but it changed the collective experiences of millions of people and her story is now generally common knowledge and represents more than she originally planned. Malala represents a movement for education now – something far more than a need for her own education and those of the girls around her.

Malala managed to energise people's positive qualities and engender support from people despite them also facing hostile social and community zealotry and a complex political situation. We read of others' experiences in trying to create positive social change such as Benazir Bhutto who was assassinated and the murders of others who speak out. It is no coincidence that Malala chooses to wear 'one of Benazir Bhutto's white shawls' when she speaks to the United Nations. Individuals often refuse to speak out because of fear and social pressure, while others maintain their views despite this. We see these interesting contrasts in how people relate to the experiences they have.

We also can reflect on the collective experiences of the Pakistani people as they fight to overcome natural disasters such as the massive earthquake and the flooding which devastated the whole country. In these instances we can see how some reach out to help others selflessly while others take the situation and twist it to their own advantage, such as the Taliban. These incidents also show the collective will of different cultures who came together to help the Pakistani victims despite being under some threat themselves. This shows the emotional bond and connectedness people feel to each other despite many differences.

Malala's father, Ziauddin Yousafzai, is always part of her experience and is a great example of an individual experience that shows how a person can maintain their individual ethics and morality in the face of great odds and personal danger. He relies on his own religious and moral code and can support it, as he does when faced with questioning. He doesn't make assumptions about the world but continues to question and stand up for what he believes. We can also consider here the changes in Malala's mother who also begins to change and adapt to her new existence despite being homesick for Swat. One example is allowing her photo to be taken and her striving to become literate.

We can also see the fragility of human experiences and how circumstances can alter everything. These connected experiences can affect many despite being from different cultures. One example is the 9/11 terror attacks which changed the American collective experience but also had repercussions around the world. As Malala says,

> 'We did not realise then that 9/11 would change our world too, and would bring war into our valley.' (p46)

The war that comes to Swat is both a collective and individual experience and while it affects all in terms of experience people respond to it in different ways. For example many initially give the Taliban money and resources as they come under the guise of religion but as events unfold many realise their true motivation and come to resent their presence and interference in everyday life. This is a very different war to the one Malala wants to wage. Her battle is against ignorance and prejudice and she says after seeing the girl selling 'oranges',

> 'I took a photo of her and vowed I would do everything in my power to help educate girls just like her. This was the war I was going to fight.' (p182)

In Pashtun life, there is a rich cultural tradition and heritage of stories and ways of interacting. This is established early in the text and continuously throughout. Initially Malala tells us the historical resonance of her name,

'I was named after Malalai of Maiwand, the greatest heroine of Afghanistan. Pashtuns are a proud people of many tribes split between Pakistan and Afghanistan. We live as we have for centuries by a code called *Pashtunwali*, which obliges us to give hospitality to all guests and in which the most important value is *nang* or honour' (p10)

The concept of honour is strong and it is common across all cultures but it is particularly strong here and ingrained. The stories Malala relates in the text reflect the times and culture of the collective experience of the Pashtun peoples and the historical relevance of it to modern living. It also reflects on the Pashtun idea of independence and what differentiates them from others, creating a stronger identity. We see this in Malala's desire to return home several times despite being in danger and, even at the conclusion of her story, she hungers to return to her 'home' when it is safe. Place cannot be excluded from her experience.

We can also read how similar collective experiences can be interpreted differently. One example is the manner in which the Quran has different meanings to various groups. The Taliban adopt an archaic literal and extreme interpretation, whereby women are excluded from any education. But, as Malala states,

'The Taliban could take our pens and books, but they couldn't stop our minds from thinking.' (p122)

As Malala's father says it is about interpretation and she doesn't have to follow the belief system of her *qari sahib* (Islamic studies teacher). He tells her,

'don't follow his explanations and interpretation. Only learn what God says. His words are divine messages, which you are free and independent to interpret.' (p111)

This religious book is a collective experience but we see many interpretations as we do in the text and the world around us today. We see this in Malala's discussions of the Sunni and Shia branches of Islam,

> 'We Muslims are split between Sunni and Shias – we share the same fundamental beliefs and the same Holy Quran but we disagree who is the right person to lead our religion...' p76

as well as other interpretations. We also see the Islamification program of General Zia and the more modern approaches of educated, intelligent leaders in Pakistan. Everyone has and uses their different experiences to place an interpretation on events,. This is part of human nature and we, to some extent, are all products of the human experiences we have.

Islam and Education

Religion is central to human experience in *I Am Malala*. The religion of Pakistan is overwhelmingly Muslim and the country was 'born' as a Muslim homeland. It is at the core of Pakistanis' lives and central to their experiences, indeed much of their cultural experience is based upon religious ceremonies and rites. Malala herself is deeply religious and she observes and maintains the correct rituals and rules of her beliefs. She writes about education,

> 'Islam too has given us this right. Islam says every girl and boy should go to school. In the Quran it is written, God wants us to have knowledge.' (p263)

The Taliban take a different view and their interpretation denies women the right to education. They back up their words with brutal ferocity,

'The most shocking attack was in June in the city of Quetta when a suicide bomber blew up a bus taking forty pupils to their all-girls college. Fourteen of them were killed. The wounded were followed to hospital and some nurses shot.' (p264)

The need for education in a country where illiteracy is statistically so high is obvious. Human experiences and the quality of life can be dramatically altered by education, so we would assume some consensus on this. Yet, as we have discussed earlier, it is the experiences and ways of reacting to those experiences that shapes people's views of the world. We need to seek to understand, individually and collectively, the motivations for these reactions and the assumptions they lead to, especially so when they are designed to deny individuals, groups or, in this case, genders a denial of basic human rights.

Malala's story is based on fighting the denial of these rights and the price she has paid for it. We need to remember in her story that it isn't Islam that is the problem it is the radical interpretations of it, as she clearly points out. Using religion is one way of framing her story and the human experience(s) that accompany it.

Journey as Human Experience

Another way of framing Malala's story is explaining her experiences in terms of the journey. In this we can include the journey that she takes others along with her, including family and friends. It is to be remembered that it isn't just the physical journeys such as her shooting and recovery or the travel to England, but the intellectual and spiritual journeys that accompany her fight for education.

It is interesting to note here that Malala thinks she has been consistent and thinks intuitively,

'I am Malala. My world has changed but I have not.' (p265)

Here she is referring to how she sees herself and her goals, but in reality she has changed from the little girl who just wanted to go to school and get an education. She learns to speak effectively publicly, endure physical and emotional pain, deal with critical situations and people of import while she also develops an ability to remain humble. Malala's experiential journey takes her away from her comfort zone and into a new world – one that has problems as well as plaudits.

As she journeys and undergoes these experiences, she takes her family and friends on a similar journey which enables them to develop as well. Her experiences also bring them into conflict with other people's experiences and some negative experiences. One example is that her father's life is under threat because he too is outspoken against the Taliban and refuses to bow to pressure and physical threat.

Consider looking at the human experiences in the text in terms of a journey, even if you frame it as a continuum which is the simplest manner in which to examine a journey.

Questions on Ideas

- Do you think Malala's story is a good example of human experiences? Support your ideas with evidence from the text.
- Why do you think Malala's experiences resonated around the world? What is common with people that unites them with her experiences, despite most of us never being shot!
- Discuss how Islam and various interpretations of Islam affect the experiences in the text. Use TWO specific characters to explicitly highlight points in your discussion.
- Analyse the discussion of violence in the text as conducted by the Taliban. Do you think this discussion is appropriate in the context of the text? Find some examples of the concept of the journey as human experience in the text. Think about
  - Physical journeys
  - Emotional journeys
  - Intellectual journeys
  - Imaginative journeys
- Do you think that the concept of the journey is useful in your study of human experiences? Explain your response fully.

THE ESSAY

The essay consists of the basic form of an introduction, body paragraphs and conclusion. The esssay has been the subject of numerous texts and you should have the basic form well in hand. As teachers, the point we would emphasise would be to link the paragraphs both to each other and back to your argument (which should directly respond to the question). Of course, ensure your argument is logical and sustained.

Make sure you use specific examples and that your quotes are accurate. To ensure that you respond to the question, make sure you plan carefully and are sure what relevant point each paragraph is making. It is solid technique to actually 'tie up' each point by explicitly coming back to the question.

When composing an essay the basic conventions of the form are:

> - State your argument, outline the points to be addressed and perhaps have a brief definition.

> **A solid structure for each paragraph is:**
> - Topic sentence (*the main idea and its link to the previous paragraph/ argument*)
> - Explanation/ discussion of the point including links between texts if applicable.
> - Detailed evidence (*Close textual reference – quotes, incidents and technique discussion.*)
> - Tie up by restating the point's relevance to argument/ question

> - Summary of points
> - Final sentence that restates your argument

As well as this basic structure, you will need to focus on:

Audience – for the essay the audience must be considered formal unless specifically stated otherwise. Therefore, your language must reflect the audience. This gives you the opportunity to use the jargon and vocabulary that you have learnt in English. For the audience ensure your introduction is clear and has impact. Avoid slang or colloquial language including contractions (like 'doesn't', 'e.g.', 'etc.').

Purpose – the purpose of the essay is to answer the question given. The examiner evaluates how well you can make an argument and understand the module's issues and its text(s). An essay is solidly structured so its composer can analyse ideas. This is where you earn marks. It does not retell the story or state the obvious.

Communication – Take a few minutes to plan the essay. If you rush into your answer it is almost certain you will not make the most of the brief 40 minutes to show all you know about the question. More likely you will include irrelevant details that do not gain you marks but waste your precious time. Remember an essay is formal so **do not** do the following: story-tell, list and number points, misquote, use slang or colloquial language, be vague, use non-sentences or fail to address the question.

PLAN:

Don't even think about starting without one!

Introduce... the texts you are using in the response *Argument*: The human experience is affected by: • Idea One • Idea Two • Idea Three	You need to let the marker know what texts you are discussing. You can start with a definition but it can come in the first paragraph of the body. You MUST state your argument in response to the question and the points you will cover as part of it. Wait until the end of the response to give it!

↓

Idea One – Aspect of human experience as outlined in the textual material, e.g. physical impact. **Idea Two –** Another aspect of human experience as outlined in the textual material, e.g. psychological impact. • explain the idea • where and how is it shown in the prescribed text? • where and how is it shown in related text 1? **Idea Three** – People's sense of experience is affected by context and environment • explain the idea • where and how shown in the prescribed text? • where and how shown in related text 1?	You can use the things you have learned to organise the essay. For each one, you say where you saw this in your prescribed text and where in related text(s). Two or three ideas are usually enough as you can explore them in detail.

↓

• Summary of two key ideas • Final sentence that restates your argument	Make sure your conclusion restates your argument. It does not have to be too long.

MODEL ESSAY OUTLINE

> **To what extent are human experiences significant in the set text?**
>
> **From your studies respond to this question using your set text and at least ONE piece of other textual material**

This essay needs to be attacked in a manner that responds to the question and shows ALL your knowledge about the text. The question lends itself to a close study of Malala Yousafzai & Christina Lamb's *I am Malala* as the text does show how the human experience is integral to life and how it shapes our other experiences and interaction with the world.

An introduction might be written:

> Human experiences are important in Yousafzai & Lamb's non-fiction memoir *I am Malala* and the two related texts Lawrence's film *Jindabyne* and Ed Sheeran's song *Castle on the Hill*. These texts show how human experiences are integral to human existence and bring more meaning to one's life. Life is about experiences that challenge us and define how we see the world. They shape our beliefs and attitudes and can be confronting at the same time. Without experiences our lives would be empty and meaningless.

Your essay should then follow the outlined plan and develop these ideas. This gives you the opportunity to link the texts and fully develop each of the ideas.

ANNOTATED RELATED MATERIAL: DIFFERENT STUDIES OF HUMAN EXPERIENCES

Jindabyne – Ray Lawrence

Jindabyne is an Australian film that captures a wide array of human experiences. It touches on the ideas mentioned in the introduction to this text in a number of detailed instances. We can begin by considering the following before beginning a detailed examination of the narrative.

The collective human experience:

- Aboriginality and the spiritual;
- The Fishermen and their code;
- The reaction of the townsfolk;
- Media response;
- Interaction with the natural world.

Individual Experience:

- An individual character's response to the body – choose one;
- The killer;
- Response to the revelations;
- Past experiences and how they impact on current experiences;
- Reaction to loss – emotional;
- Assumptions about life.

We can now look at the plot to help us understand each of these issues. *Jindabyne* begins with the sound of a radio being tuned and the Australian feel of the movie is immediate with the theme music for the ABC news. Lawrence emphasises the isolation by having the radio not tune in correctly for an unknown female character, forcing her to use the cassette player. With this unusual beginning we know that her experience is not going to be positive.

We then pan to the rocks slowly where Gregory, our killer, sits patiently in a truck with the engine running watching the road. We know he is prepared for this as he has binoculars. He sees an Aboriginal girl, Susan O'Connor, driving and she is the one fiddling with the radio. He chases her down and forces her to stop. He moves toward her as we see a long shot of how isolated they are. We see his face in her window looming above her and screaming about the electricity coming down from the mountains. This film is no murder mystery, as we know from the beginning that the murderer is Gregory the electrician. This is about the experiences of the other characters in the film and how they respond to current experiences.

The Kane family, Stewart, Claire and son Tom, is waking. Claire pretends to sleep, before waking suddenly and being affectionate with Tom. Stewart and Tom head out fishing. The scene doesn't feel quite right and there is some emotional tension between Stewart and Claire that is unspoken due to what they have experienced in the past. Claire had a complicated past when she was pregnant with Tom. When she finds she is pregnant again, she becomes emotional and slightly unstable.

As the film builds we see the complex pasts of the characters and their interactions in the confinement of the small town. The fishing trip is a break from this and extremely important in their lives.

We see some of the emotional instability in characters such as Caylin-Calandria, who with Tom, has some issues at school. Along with Caylin-Calandria, Claire and Jude also have issues but in a nicely framed shot of the three female characters, we see them conform as members of a close knit group. The sacrifice they make is similar to Gregory's but on a different scale. Note the connection here and how each one is to get back to order and societal norms. This is the collective experience for all the characters.

At the Kanes' home the tensions are obvious from their past experiences but they contain it for appearances' sake. Occasionally, the tension reaches breaking point and the experience strains the superficial approach. The tension builds at home and the fishing trip seems like a good opportunity to break the cycle.

When we see Gregory dump Susan O'Connor's body in the river, we know that the fishing and her death will interact.

The next morning, the fishermen head off for their one big trip of the year and the sign 'Gone fishing' is put in the garage window. We see Billy on the phone to Elissa and putting the sign the wrong way round in the window shows his immaturity. They have already said they are taking him away to make a man of him. The four men have a few beers on the way and talk as they travel through the landscape. They intend to give Billy the experience they think he needs as a 'man' — a cultural rite of passage.

The men arrive and the high-tension electricity wires punctuate the wilderness. They begin to hike toward the valley. It's a long walk in and the terrain is hilly and difficult. They stop on the way and again we see Billy's naivety when Stewart says 'Listen to that' meaning the silence but he can't, as he has his earphones in. It is part of the break in tension of the film that they commune with nature. This experiential break affects all the men. The episode represents a distinct human experience.

Stewart wanders down the river fishing and sees Susan's body caught in the rocks. Hesitantly, he wades out to it and turns it over saying 'Oh Jesus' repeatedly. He screams for the others to come as he drags the body to the bank. He is obviously upset, making the sign of the cross. Stewart tells Rocco to 'take her, for fuck's sake, take her' and their shock is obvious. They all stare at the body and Billy goes to run off but they stop him. The four men meet and decide to leave her in the water and tie her so she doesn't float away.

The presence of the body threatens to detract from the enjoyment of the fishing experience. The act of attempted isolation of the bad experience is expected to evoke only a mild response. They do not anticipate the stormy reaction it receives when they return to the community.

The men go on fishing, with Stewart getting the first big fish on an absolutely perfect day. The lure of the fish is strong, especially when they see the big one he has caught. They have a successful and enjoyable time, a positive experience. They get a photo of the catch and Billy holds up his fish in a typical hunter/gatherer pose. Capturing an experience this way is most enjoyable.

It is a photo that will come back to haunt them as things change back in the world. An unanticipated adverse reaction can be a horrific experience.

Stewart goes to check on the dead girl, rolling her over and getting debris off her face in a quite tender gesture. The next day they head back and report it. At the car Billy rings Elissa and says they found a body but 'caught the most amazing fish'. They are told by the police to wait and seem despondent their trip has been ruined. They organise their story as Stewart says they have 'to get their story straight'.

We cut to Gregory eating breakfast and he appears to be a normal, lonely man until he goes out to his shed where he has hidden Susan's car and this reminds us of the evil in him. Consider his experience and his motivations. How does he see his actions and the world?

The next day at the station the policeman tells the fishermen 'we don't step over bodies for our recreational pursuits' and 'the whole town's ashamed of you'. When they are told to 'piss off' from the station the press are waiting for them and Billy makes a comment. Carl is angry with the press but we can begin to see signs of distress within the whole group.

The experience they had so looked forward to has become a negative one and the tensions we saw before are exacerbated by the emotional and collective response to the murder. Claire soon becomes obsessed with the whole affair because of her own state. The newspaper the next day has the headline, 'Men fish over dead body' because Billy has talked. Billy is late to work and Stewart tells him they have to 'stick together on this'.

Susan's sister calls them 'animals' and raises the race question by asking if they would have left a white girl. The Aboriginal youths begin to attack and vandalise the property of the men in violent outbursts, including throwing a rock through Billy's van window and thus endangering his baby. They insult Carl at the caravan park and vandalise the garage.

The police aren't any help and the situation deteriorates. Jude tells the police they shouldn't be enforcing the 'political correctness' laws. The intervention of the sense of Aboriginality and race challenges the assumptions people have and how we see the world. The contrasting views are ingrained in the social structures and part of different collective experiences.

The Aboriginal people see the white people as 'interfering' and the group of fishermen begin to fight amongst themselves. Elissa says they shouldn't go to the bush at all as it's sacred. The group talk about the bush and Rocco punches Stewart for saying the Aborigines are superstitious. The experience of racial tension becomes ever-present and adds to the emotional responses to the experience.

We now head slowly to a resolution of the conflict brought about by the various experiences. Each is handled in a different manner by characters and you can explore one or two of the responses. To cycle back to the original murder, Claire is stalked by Gregory in his truck. He stops her but drives off after staring weirdly, an odd experience in itself.

Terry and Stewart talk and Stewart meets Rocco and Carl. He tells them Claire's left him 'again'. Rocco can't believe it and we cross cut to her looking out into the wilderness after he looks thoughtfully out the window. These different reactions to experiences mirror attitudes in life and reactions to emotional and intellectual conflict.

In conclusion, Lawrence takes us back to the healing power of nature in our human experiences when the Aboriginal people are having a ceremony. Gregory watches while Claire walks in. Again we see his truck as an omnipresent force in the film, almost an extension of him. An Aboriginal man tells Claire to 'piss off' from the ceremony after she says she has come to pay her 'respects' but he is told to leave her alone by an Auntie.

The smoke and tribal music symbolise the ceremonial nature of the setting and the camera pans around the scene and the bush. We see parts of the ceremony with chanting and clapping sticks. The camera moves in and out while other shots pan around the bush, giving us the full experience and Lawrence portrays this as a positive, healing experience.

Eventually Stewart, Tom, Carl, Jude and Rocco arrive to pay respects. Tom runs to his mother and Stewart goes over and says 'Sorry' but is rebuffed by the father who throws dirt on him and spits, refusing his apology. Then an Aboriginal girl tells a little about Susan's story and sings the last love song Susan wrote.

The camera pans around all the faces as they listen to the song and the ceremonial smoke wafts around. It seems to have some healing effect on everyone, as it is a meaningful experience which raises the idea of the spiritual experience in the text. The girl stops singing through emotion. 'Be gone' seems to symbolise in language the whole scenario for each character.

We see a long wide shot of the bush before fading back to Gregory waiting again in his car behind the rocks for another victim. It is quite a circular conclusion and it is an odd end when he crushes the fly. We don't quite know what to make of the whole experience and he seems to be the only character unchanged by the experiences in the film.

Poem: 'Inland' by John Kinsella

The poem captures the mood and ethos of the outback farming communities and deals with the human aspect more than some of the other poems in Kinsella's collection: *Peripheral Light*. This poem is one long restless thought that mimics memories and recollection while raising the current, topical issues that concern the poet. As usual with his poems Kinsella orientates the audience early with the word 'Inland' and then continues the poem without a full stop. The poem flows with the use of commas but Kinsella allows us to stop and think with the use of the colon, brackets and the hyphen. Look for these punctuation stops as you read as they emphasise a specific point or idea that resonates with the audience.

The first stanza gives us a foreshadowing of the events to follow with the warnings in the words 'storm', 'alert' and 'uncertain'. This ominous tone is reinforced by the word 'ghosts' and the implication of death which is constant in much of Kinsella's poetry. The next stanza deals with a more human element and we get the country feel with the bracketed gossip about McHenry's accident which shows the close knit community. Habits here are formed as part of survival and known to all as we see 'the old man plying the same track' and the families possibly heading to church on the Sunday morning.

The third stanza returns to the vagaries of nature. Kinsella repeats 'uncertain' with regard to the weather. Weather and the environment play a large role in farming communities and it is especially so at sowing and harvest. Despite the uncertainty and 'ashen' days which alter 'moods', the community returns to their habits and routines which shape their lives. The next stage returns to the road and the implication of a journey but a journey that is straight and in conflict with the cycles of the natural world. The path seems already marked and measured. It is 'straight and narrow', marked by a theodolite.

The final four lines of the poem are pure Kinsella, marking the transience of humanity on the landscape. We read

> 'it's a place of borrowed dreams
> where the marks of the spirit
> have been erased by dust –
> the restless topsoil'

The European farmers had 'borrowed dreams' for their own relationship with the land but this line also harks back to the indigenous Dreamtime when the land was created. The indigenous view that the land owns the people is also true for Kinsella. This sense of nobody owning the land is strong in his poetry. European impact on the land can be seen in the spirituality being removed by the dust — dust created by the poor farming techniques transferred from a different land. He finishes with the 'restless topsoil' as if the whole earth is moving in its own discontented journey, just as the people move.

The influence here of genuinely lost spirituality and connection with the land as we move directly on the 'high road' contrasts with the more flowing, 'restless' side of the natural world. This visual contrast is obvious but we can also discuss the contrast between habit and spirit. 'Inland' is a poem that uses the landscape to show the contrast between two views of the countryside.

DRAMA: Eugene O'Neil's *Desire Under the Elms*

O'Neill sets out to instruct how the house and elms should appear and the year is 1850. Note how he describes the 'enormous' elms as,

> 'exhausted women resting their sagging breasts and
> hands and hair on its roof, and when it rains their tears
> trickle down monotonously and rot on the shingles'

and how they dominate and 'rot'. It is important to read this both in terms of the play and in the context of American theatre. The description here shows O'Neill's genius at new design and original theatricality.

Part One: Scene One

The whole first page and a third are nearly all playwright notes that describe the farm, the house and the characters of Eben, Simeon and Peter. The first words of the play, 'God! Purty!' reflect the beauty of the land and how Eben perceives it. Eben is 'resentful and defensive' and feels 'trapped' on the farm.

His older half-brothers Simeon and Peter are 'more bounce and homelier in face, shrewder and more practical.' They all have worked hard on their father's farm over the years and have little feeling for their absent father. We learn that Simeon had a 'woman' who died and that Peter is excited by the prospect of 'gold in the West'. They all talk about how hard they've worked and hope that the father might 'die soon'. What we get from all this is that they are earthy and this is reflected in their bodies and clothes which are all dirt stained.

We also see here the difference between them as Eben sees gold in the pasture, not California, as they head in for a dinner of bacon in what seems a ritual they have performed many times before. Note that O'Neill calls for the use of the curtain at the end of the scene.

Scene Two

It is twilight and again we get detailed notes on the interior scene. Simeon tells Eben he should not wish their father dead and Eben replies he's not his son but, 'I'm Maw – every drop of blood!' He then blames the father, Ephraim Cabot, for killing his mother by working her to death but the others just say there was work to be done. O'Neill gets them to list the jobs and Eben comes back with 'vengeful passion' that, while they did nothing, he will see his mother gets 'rest and sleep in her grave!'

They then discuss Cabot's absence and how he just drove off in a buggy one day in a rush. Simeon says that when he went,

> 'He druv off in the buggy, all spick an' span, with the mare all breshed an' shiny, druv off clackin' his tongue an' wavin' his whip. I remember it quite well'

Eben mocks Simeon for not stopping him and the scene concludes with Eben leaving to see Minnie the town whore. We learn all the Cabot men have slept with her. Simeon and Peter say that Eben is just like 'Paw' and thinks of California. The final image is of Eben with his arms stretched to the sky talking about starts and sin, 'my sin's as purty as any one on 'em!', until he 'strides' to the village for Min.

Scene Three

It is 'pitch darkness' and Eben comes home with the news that Cabot has married a 'purty' thirty-five year old. He has heard this in the village and this effectively disinherits the boys. Simeon and Peter see California as their only option now. Eben tells the boys that they can have three hundred dollars each if they sign their share of the farm over to him. He can get the money as his mother told him,

> 'I know whar it's hid. I been waitin' – Maw told me. She knew whar it lay fur years, but she was waitin'....It's her'n – the money he hoarded from her farm an' hid from Maw. It's my money by rights now.'

They think about it and Eben tells them about his night with Min. He tells how he hates the new wife after the boys suggest he might sleep with her, just like Min, to get the old man back. Peter and Simeon say they'll do the deal and leave the farm. Both are bitter and vindictive about Cabot.

Scene Four

The setting is the same as Scene Two and the boys are discussing how they don't have to work now – it is all down to Eben who is jubilant as he thinks it will all be his. Peter and Simeon again reflect on how like his father he is, 'Like his Paw'. They also tell he isn't much of a milker but they soon talk about their leaving and how they'll miss some aspects of the farm.

Eben comes back in and says that the 'old mule an the bride' are coming. The two older boys begin to pack and sign Eben's papers as he gives them the money Cabot had hidden. They tell him they'll send him 'a lump o' gold for Christmas' and head into the yard feeling 'light' because of their newfound freedom.

Ephraim Cabot and Abbie Putnam then come in and O'Neill describes them in detail. Cabot is

> 'seventy-five, tall and gaunt, with great, wiry, concentrated power, but stoop shouldered by toil. His face is hard as if it were hewn from a boulder, yet there is a weakness in it'

but his face is weakened with petty pride. Abbie is

> 'thirty-five, buxom, full of vitality. Her round face is pretty but marred by its rather gross sensuality. There is strength and obstinacy in her jaw, a hard determination in her eyes, and about her whole personality.'

She also has a 'desperate quality'. Cabot shows Abbie the place and she says to him it's 'mine'. Then he sees the two boys not working. He introduces Abbie and she goes to look at 'her' house and they warn her Eben's inside.

Cabot tells them to get to work and they give him cheek, saying they are 'free' and heading to California. They 'whoop' it up and he says he'll have them chained up. They throw rocks at the house, smashing the window and head off singing. Abbie sticks her head out the window and says she likes the room but he is thinking of the stock and 'almost runs' to the barn.

Abbie then meets Eben in the kitchen and talks to him in 'seductive tones'. She says she doesn't want to be his 'Maw' but friends and he cusses her. She tells him of her troubled life and how Cabot gave her a chance to escape it. He calls her a 'harlot' and they argue over ownership of the farm. She has the upper hand in law and he leaves but the seeds of their growing attraction have been set.

Outside he and his father argue about life and work and he tells Eben 'Ye'll never be more'n half a man!' The scene ends with Abbie washing up and the faint notes of the song the boys were singing as they left.

Part Two: Scene One

Again O'Neill describes in detail the farmhouse setting. Two months have passed and it is a hot Sunday afternoon. Abbie in her best outfit is sitting on the porch and Eben comes out of the house also dressed in his best. They stalk each other, both attracted and repelled. As he walks away she 'gives a sneering, taunting chuckle' at him and they argue but the attraction is obvious. She says that nature will pull him to her but he says that she is married and he goes to leave her.

She accuses him of going to Min and she gets angry stating he'll never get the farm,

> 'Ye'll never live t' see the day when even a stinkin' weed on
> it 'll belong t' ye!'

He says he hates her and leaves as Cabot enters. She tells him Eben has been mocking him and twists the conversation to the inheritance of the farm. She tells him Eben lusts after her and as he angers she backs off in her accusations. Reassured, he says that she can have the farm if she bears the son she says she wants with him. He says that he'd 'do anythin' ye axed, I tell ye!' if she gave him a son and tells her to pray to God for it to happen.

Scene Two

It is about eight in the evening and here the bedrooms are highlighted, with Eben in one and Cabot with Abbie in the other. The two of them are talking about a son. They seem together, yet apart, as he tells her of his life on the farm and how God's hard. He both lost and gained on the way through, but the farm is his. He says he is pleased he found her, his 'Rose o' Sharon'. Abbie promises him that she will bear a son as he basically threatens her,

> 'Ye don't know nothin' – nor never will. If ye don't hev a son t' redeem ye...'

and he leaves to sleep in the barn with the cows 'whar it's restful'.

We then see Eben and Abbie restless and she leaves the room and goes to him. He 'submits' to her kisses then 'hurls' her away. Abbie says she'd make him 'happy' and she knows he wants her too much. She tells him to go down to the parlour and he is shocked as this is where his mother was 'laid out'. She leaves for the parlour and he wonders what's happening. The scene closes with a question to his dead mother, 'Maw! Whar are yew?' but we know that he wants her and will go to her.

Scene Three

The scene now shifts to the parlour which is described as a 'grim, repressed room like a tomb'. Abbie waits and Eben appears and he sits at her invitation. They talk about his Maw and how they hate Cabot. Abbie throws herself at him with 'wild passion' and he is caught up in the moment and thinks that it's his Maw wanting him to sleep with Abbie to get revenge on Cabot,

I see it! I sees why. It's her vengeance on him – so's she kin rest quiet in her grave!

Abbie proclaims her love for him and he for her then they kiss 'in a fierce, bruising kiss' to close the scene.

Scene Four

A more bold and confident Eben leaves the house and Abbie opens the parlour window. She calls him over for a kiss and they talk a bit before Eben says his Maw can now rest. They split as Cabot comes out of the barn but are now obviously in love. Eben tells Cabot that his Maw is now at rest and Cabot says he rests best with the cows. Cabot is confused but the scene ends with him criticising Eben as 'Soft-headed' and a 'born fool' but, being a practical man, he heads for breakfast.

Part Three: Scene One

Time has passed to 'late spring the following year'. Eben is upstairs in emotional and psychological conflict while a party happens downstairs. Cabot has drunk too much and Abbie sits, pale and thin, in a rocking chair. There is a fiddler and Abbie begins the scene by asking for Eben and the guests 'titter' as most think the baby is Eben's, not Cabot's, which is true enough. They laugh and Cabot is angered by this and orders them to dance. The fiddler 'slyly' says they're waiting for Eben but Cabot mocks the boy and then ensues a bawdy conversation about his fertility,

I got a lot in me – a hell of a lot – folks don't know on. Fiddle 'er up, durn ye! Give 'em somethin' t' dance t!'

The fiddler plays and they dance. Cabot joins in frantically and 'whoop(s)' it up. He exhausts the fiddler and pours whiskey. In the upstairs room Eben is looking at the baby. Abbie goes upstairs and Cabot leaves for outside, 'fresh air', as she has told him not to 'tech' her. The guests gossip after he goes and we see Eben and Abbie upstairs and she professes her love for him,

> 'Don't git feelin' low. I love ye, Eben. Kiss me.'

Cabot says he's going to rest in the barn. The scene concludes with the fiddler playing in celebration of 'the old skunk gittin' fooled!'

Scene Two

Eben is outside half an hour later and Cabot is coming back from the barn. Cabot tells him to get a woman inside and he might get a farm. Eben replies that this farm's his and Cabot mocks him. He tells her Abbie has been promised the farm for her son and Eben is angered thinking Abbie has tricked him.

Eben goes to kill her but Cabot is too strong for him and Abbie comes out to stop him choking Eben. Cabot tells him he's weak and goes inside to celebrate. Abbie tries to be tender with Eben but he rejects her and calls her a liar.

> 'Ye're nothin' but a stinkin' passel o' lies. Ye've been lyin'
> t' me every word ye spoke, day an' night, since we fust –
> done it. Ye've kept sayin' ye loved me....'

She says she loves him and tells him that the promise was made before they fell in love. He says he'll go to California.

They argue and he 'torturedly' says he wished the baby had never been born. Abbie is distraught and she says she'd kill the baby to prove her love for him. He says he won't listen to her but she calls after him that she can 'prove' she loves him and she 'kin do one thin' God does'. Abbie is desperate at the end of the scene.

Scene Three

It is now just before dawn and Eben is in the kitchen ready to leave. Abbie is near the cradle with 'her face full of terror'. She sobs but Cabot stirs and she goes to the kitchen and flings her arms around Eben, kissing him 'wildly'. She says 'I killed him' and he thinks she means Cabot but is horrified when she tells him it's the baby.

Eben states it was his baby and she says she loved it but loves him more. He is angered,

> 'Don't ye tech me! Ye're pizzen! How could ye – t' murder a pore little critter – Ye must've swapped yer soul t' hell!

and tells her that he is getting the Sheriff and heads, 'panting and sobbing' to town. She calls out to him that she loves him.

Scene Four

It is after dawn and Abbie is in the kitchen. Cabot wakes in his room and is concerned that he has woken late. He checks the baby and is proud it is quiet and asleep. He goes down to Abbie in the kitchen and she tells him the baby is dead. He runs to check and comes back down and asks 'why?'

In a rage she tells him it was Eben's son and that she loves Eben, not him. He blinks back a tear and then gets 'stony' so he can carry on and says he is going to get the Sheriff. Abbie tells him that Eben's already gone so that Cabot tells her he'll 'git t' wuk.' He then tells her he'd never have told and now he's going to be 'lonesomer'n ever!' Eben comes back and Cabot tells him to get off the farm.

Eben asks for her forgiveness and tells her he loves her. He says he realised he loved her at the Sheriff's and they have a chance to run away but Abbie says she'll take her punishment. Eben says he will share it with her and plans to tell the Sheriff they planned it together. They think they can stand it together and then Cabot comes back.

He goes into a long tirade and tells them how he's let the stock go and will burn the house down. He too plans to go to California but finds that Eben has gotten to his money first. Cabot says that this is a sign from God to him to stay and that 'God's hard an' lonesome!' At this point the Sheriff comes and Eben says he was involved with the baby's murder.

Cabot says 'Take 'em both' and leaves to get his stock. The sun is coming up and as they are led away Eben says the farm's 'Purty' and Abbie agrees. The Sheriff finishes the play with the line, 'It's a jim-dandy farm, no denyin'. Wish I owned it!'

OTHER RELATED TEXTS

Fiction / Non-fiction / Drama

- *Wonder* – R G Palacio
- *First they Killed My Father* – Luong Ung
- *The Graveyard Book* – Neil Gaiman
- *Looking for Alaska* – John Green
- *Eleanor and Park* by Rainbow Rowell
- *The Fault in Our Stars* – John Green
- *We All Fall Down* – Robert Cormier
- *The Old Man and the Sea* – Ernest Hemingway
- *The Fire Eaters* – David Almond
- *Ender's Game* – Orson Scott Card
- *Hatchet* – Gary Paulsen
- *Inside Black Australia* – Kevin Gilbert
- *Sapiens: A Brief History of Humankind* – Yuval Noah Harari
- *Peeling the Onion* – Wendy Orr
- *Raw* – Scott Monk
- *Six Degrees of Separation* – John Guare
- *The Book Thief* – Markus Zusak
- *When Dogs Cry* – Markus Zusak
- *Holes* – Louis Sachar
- *The Outsiders* – S.E. Hinton
- *Roll of Thunder, Hear My Cry* – Mildred D. Taylor
- *A Small Free Kiss in the Dark* – Glenda Millard
- *Monster* – Walter Dean Myers
- *Lord of the Flies* – William Golding
- *Jandamarra* – Steve Hawke
- *A Separate Peace* – John Knowles
- *A Monster Calls* – Patrick Ness
- *The Pigman* – Paul Zindel
- *The Invention of Hugo Cabret* – Brian Selznik

- *Emerald City* – David Williamson
- *Silent Spring* – Rachel Carson

Films and Television

- *The Human Experience* – Charles Kinnane
- *My Brilliant Career* – Gillian Armstrong
- *Broadchurch* – James Strong & Euros Lyn
- *Twinsters* – Samantha Futerman and Ryan Miyamoto
- *Be My Brother* – Genevieve Clay - Smith
- *What's Eating Gilbert Grape* – Lasse Hallstrom
- *Pleasantville* – Gary Ross
- *Eternal Sunshine of the Spotless Mind* – Michel Gondry
- *Taxi Driver* – Martin Scorsese
- *Tootsie* – Sydney Pollack
- *Back in Time for Dinner* – Kim Maddever
- *The Godfather* – Francis Ford Coppola
- *Friends* – David Crane and Marta Kaufmann
- *Dawson's Creek* – Kevin Williamson
- *Orange is the New Black* – Jenji Kohan
- *Boy Meets World* – Michael Jacobs and April Kelly

Website – quote on literature and the human experience

http://view2.fdu.edu/academics/university-college/school-of-humanities/
english-language-and-literature-program/

At its most fundamental level literature explores what it means to be a human being in this world and tries to describe what our human experience is like. As such, literature pushes us to confront the large human questions that have plagued humankind for centuries: issues of fate and free will, issues relating to our role in the universe, our relationship to God, and our relationships with others. Studying literature not only helps us to understand the complexity of these questions intellectually, but because of its very nature, it allows us to experience these tensions vicariously. Literature does not just tell us about human experience; it recreates it in a way we can feel and visualise. In other words, it calls for a total response from us—it stretches us beyond who we are.

First, literature can enhance our ability to relate to people. Because literature focuses on human relationships and self perception, it can broaden our own experience—to help us understand different kinds of people, different cultures, different problems—and, consequently, help us better understand our own relationships with others.

The study of literature also helps to foster an appreciation for beauty, symmetry, and order. This means more than the intuitive response of liking or disliking something we see or read or hear; it means a carefully thought-through response that will enhance appreciation—not destroy it.

Perhaps the most important skills that the study of literature teaches are analytic and synthetic skills. In learning to read carefully and analytically, we learn to ask hard questions both of the work and of ourselves. And as we seek to discover the relationships between the ideas and images we uncover in a work, our ultimate goal is to see the whole—to see how the parts work together to make the piece what it is. In grappling with the complex and difficult ideas contained in literature, we learn to accept the multiple dimensions and ambiguity that are so often present in life.

Finally, the study of literature will also help develop our writing abilities as we come to value the written word and understand its power to communicate.

Beyond all of these skills, however, it is not what literature can do for us as individuals as much as what it can do to us. Literature speaks to the whole person. Listen to it, says C. S. Lewis, and you will be changed.

Poetry

- 'Warren Pryor' – Alden Nowlan
- 'The Gardener' – Louis MacNeice
- 'The Improvers' – Colin Thiele

Songs

- *Be My Escape* – Relient K
- *Mandolin Wind* – Rod Stewart
- *Roxanne* – The Police
- *Wake Me Up When September Ends* – Green Day
- *Under Pressure* – Queen & David Bowie
- *Candle in the Wind* – Elton John
- *Empire State of Mind* – Alicia Keys
- *Gold Digger* – Kanye West
- *We Are Young* – Fun.
- *Centrefold* – J. Geils Band
- *It's Time* – Imagine Dragons
- *We Cry* – The Script
- *If I Were a Boy* – Beyoncé
- *Shake it Out* – Florence + the Machine
- *C'mon* – Panic! At the Disco & Fun.
- *I Don't Love You* – My Chemical Romance
- *Sing* – My Chemical Romance
- *1985* – Bowling for Soup
- *What About Me* – Shannon Noll
- *Sinner* – Jeremy Loops
- *7 Years* – Lucas Graham

- *Bitter Sweet Symphony* – The Verve
- *Ghost!* – Kid Kudi
- *Good Riddance (Time of Your Life)* – Green Day
- *Expectations* – Belle and Sebastian
- *After Hours* – We Are Scientists
- *Write About Love* – Belle and Sebastian
- *Trust Your Stomach* – Marching Band
- *Heaven Knows I'm Miserable Now* – The Smiths